WOLFPACK

WOLFPACK

U-BOATS AT WAR 1939-1945

PHILIP KAPLAN AND JACK CURRIE

NAVAL INSTITUTE PRESS
ANNAPOLIS, MARYLAND

Squadron Leader Jack Currie, DFC, didn't live to see
the publication of this book. Jack was spirited, tough,
generous and thoroughly professional...a gentleman.
I am proud to have known him.
This is for you, mate.

PK

First published in 1997 by Aurum Press Ltd., 25 Bedford Avenue
London WC1B 3AT

Published and distributed in the United States of America and
Canada by the Naval Institute Press, 118 Maryland Avenue,
Annapolis, MD 21402-5035

Library of Congress Catalog Card Number: 96-70026

ISBN 1-55750-855-0

This edition is authorized for sale only in the United States, its
territories and possessions, and Canada

Printed and bound in Singapore by Imago using acid-free paper

CONTENTS

BASICALLY the sea is an unfriendly element. It carries within it large quantities of chlorine and such constituents as magnesium, potassium, fluoride and strontium, some of which are toxic and few conducive to health. Its density, which affects the way that ships—and especially submarines—behave, changes from time to time and from place to place, according to the temperature, as does the air, which similarly affects an aeroplane's performance. The sea is also intrinsically unstable, constantly varying in nature and in movement: one day calm and silent, with sunlight shining on a surface like a garden pool, the next day turbulent and clamorous beneath a lowering sky. On one day a man can see as far as there is anything to see; another day, nothing is visible beyond the next great green roller that towers above the bow. Every sailor, and every airman, who cares about his life learns to treat the element he moves in with respect, and the underwater sailor more than most: living in his narrow metal drum, he comes closer to its deeper, darker secrets, and to an understanding of its awesome power.

It was the popular belief in World War II that, in common with combat aircrew, paratroopers and commandos, all submariners were volunteers. The fact was they were not. Many a young German became an underwater sailor through an age-old Service method of selection, the order: "I want three volunteers—you, you and you." Once he was committed, however, to the Ubootwaffe, by whatever means, the "volunteer" soon became aware that he was a member of a band of brothers, a *corps d'élite*, and took pride in being so. As with the members of any close-knit unit—a commando force, an SAS squad, a heavy bomber crew—there was a camaraderie among the U-boat men, a more powerful unity and sense of interdependence than most other sailors felt. Their environment was cramped and claustrophobic, insanitary and smelly, but they were bound together by the dangers and the purpose that they shared, however ill-conceived that purpose may have been.

Another misconception fostered by the propagandists of the warring nations was that, while "our" submariners were gallant maritime adventurers, those of the enemy were ruthless murderers, skulking under water to slaughter helpless sailors. Again there was the analogy with airmen, who were either "terror fliers" and "assassins of the air", or "our brave bomber boys", depending on the point of view. The truth is there were U-boat men who, as seamen first and foremost, detested the destruction of a fine, seaworthy ship, and there were others who rejoiced; in the same way, there were bomber crewmen who rued the devastation of a splendid town, and others who had no qualms at all. But in war there was seldom any place for qualms or regrets: both U-boat and bomber crews had to do the job they had been trained for, as was expected of them by Admiral Dönitz and the Herrenvolk on one side of the Channel, and by Air Chief Marshal Harris and the British people on the other.

Basic training for the Ubootwaffe recruits, as for all German servicemen, was arduous and strict, and for the first three months they heard and saw little of seamanship or of submarines. That would come later, with their specialized training. For now, it was lectures, "square-bashing" and demanding physical training, interspersed with tests designed to eliminate all those who seemed unlikely to withstand the privations and dangers of the U-boat war.

Those who passed the training had to be the sort of men who did not mind being unaware of where or why they were going when they sailed out of harbour, who had never known claustrophobia, who could live in close proximity to forty other men for up to three months at a time and who could spend four hours on watch, lashed by icy winds, their eyes stung by salt spray, strapped or chained to a deck rail or wire to avoid being swept away, and learning the truth of the old sailor's saying that "water is pointed". As John Waters wrote in his *Bloody Winter*, "The North Atlantic is where the seaman takes his graduate course in weather, and the

FORTY-FOUR SWEATING SEAMEN

We are all in the gutter, but some of us are looking at the stars.
—Oscar Wilde

left: The engine-order telegraph of *U-505*, a Type IXC submarine on permanent display at the Museum of Science and Industry, Chicago. above: The life vest of a U-boat crewman.

Prosperity makes friends
and adversity tries them.
—Anonymous

curriculum is tough."

The men best suited for life aboard a U-boat were those who could sleep well in a bed that was still warm and redolent of the man who last lay in it, and who could stay in dreamland through the hissing of the inlet valves, the odd gurgle of the bilge-pumps and the pounding of the pistons, and who would only be awakened by the sound of depth charges or the warning klaxon. They were those who could tumble out of bed and scramble aft or forward like pieces of human ballast when the Commander ordered "Take her up" or "Dive", who would be ever keen for action (and not just because there would be more room in the fore-ends when a few eels had been fired), who could stay motionless and silent for hour after hour while the depth charges boomed around them and hurled the boat about, and who never worried when their muscles began to atrophy from insufficient exercise.

They had to be the sort of men who thought nothing of scraping a coat of mildew off their breakfast sausages, of sucking the last drop of juice out of a rotting lemon in order to ingest a modicum of vitamin C, of queueing with a bursting bladder at the solitary "head", waiting for the current occupant who had clearly gone to sleep or died in there. They had to be able to accept the outbreaks of rashes, boils or crab lice that were all part of life in a U-boat...

Their first acquaintance with the boat they were to serve in, and possibly to die in, would ideally be in the shipyard where it was being built. There, in Wilhelmshaven, Kiel, Bremen or Hamburg, they saw the way it was being constructed, learned to find their way about its narrow labyrinths, to know where all the handles, wheels and buttons were, and met their mess-mates, their officers and, above all, their Commander, who, from that time on, would share and shape their lives and most probably their fate. When the boat was completed, fitted out and painted, the shipbuilders threw a formal luncheon party for the crew before they took over the U-boat for the "working up" exercise.

Out in the proving waters of the Baltic, they made many practice dives to test the operation of the hydroplanes, and of the trim and ballast tanks, and to prove the strength of the pressure hull at depth. There were dummy launches of torpedoes, reloading practices, tests of the diesels and electric motors, of the armament, the radio and sonar. As the days went by, they got to know one another and their officers, and began to realize that, although they were all individuals, each was now a part of something more—a unit that was going to war. This was the touchstone that helped them to become the sort of men they had to be. Not so much for love of country, nor yet for love of family,

far left: The members of a commanding officers' course were trained in the Baltic for five months before being assigned to a flotilla. left: At work on hydroplane controls and depth gauges of *U-65*, a Type IXB U-boat near Brest, September 1940. next page: With the deck casing awash, a gun crew prepares their weapon for firing.

but out of loyalty to the men they had trained, messed and sailed with, and with whom they now shared their lives.

However strong the sense of crew identity, there were always some distinctions between one group and another, and not just those that were due to the hierarchy of rank. There was a clear division, for example, between the deck and the engine room, between the hardy, weather-beaten sailors of the sea-watch and the smelly, pale stokers and greasers down below, and there were subdivisions between the engine room artificers and the electricians, and between the control room hands, the telegraphists and the torpedo men, all with their own internal loyalties, by no means discouraged by their mates and petty officers. And always the Commander—"Herr Kaleu" or "The Old Man"—stood alone. His were the decisions that meant success or failure, maybe life or death, and the relationship, the depth of understanding, between him and the Chief Engineer was the most important on the boat.

Twelve patrols were expected of a U-boat man before he was assigned to non-combatant duties— an unrealistic number that, like the Allied bomber crewman's tour of twenty-five or thirty missions, gave him little chance of survival. But few men, at the time, were thinking on those lines. The oath they had taken on their enlistment pledged them to their duty and, as the British soldiers said, "If you can't take a joke, you shouldn't have joined."

The armed forces system of honours and awards has always provided an incentive for a fighting man to accept the hazards and rigours of his life. In this respect, the men of the U-boat arm certainly got their share. The brass patrol badge, showing a U-boat framed in a laurel wreath and surmounted by a swastika and the German eagle, was awarded for three missions, and Iron Crosses, 1st and 2nd Class, were liberally bestowed, with the occasional and more prestigious German Cross. In fact, although U-boat officers formed less

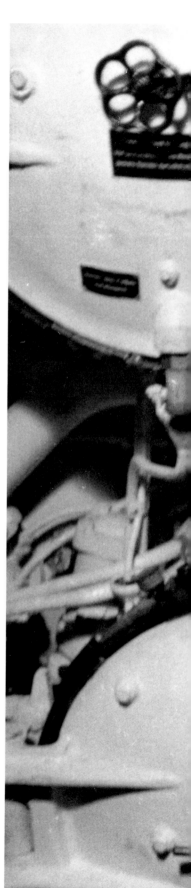

preceding page: Crewmen amid the potatoes, bread, hams, sausages and other provisions stowed for a patrol. After weeks at sea the bread became mouldy and the loaves were referred to as "white rabbits", by the crew. above: The cook on *U-373*, April 1942. above right: A meal on *U-103*, May 1942. right: Attending the diesel engines of *U-65*, a Type IXB boat near Brest, September 1940. far right: A torpedoman washes among the launching tubes in the forward torpedo room of *U-103*, May 1942.

below: The U-boat pens at Bordeaux in 1996. The complex provided fifteen sheltered berths, three of them being dry docks, and was the last of the giant U-bunker structures to be built in France.

than five per cent of the total commissioned naval strength, they received almost half of all the Knight's Crosses awarded to the Kriegsmarine. This was a distinction normally reserved for commanders who sank 100,000 tons of Allied shipping, and those who achieved 150,000 could expect the addition of the Oak Leaves; the few aces who exceeded this were rewarded with the Swords—the ultimate accolade, Diamonds (or Brilliants) were only awarded twice—once to Kapitänleutnant Albrecht Brandi, and once (deservedly) to Kapitän zur See Wolfgang Lüth.

Despite all incentives—the special rates of pay, the best of rations, the medals and the glory—by no means everybody had the stomach for warfare in a U-boat. A few bad hours lying deep in the Atlantic, gasping for breath, simultaneously shivering with fear and sweating like a pig,

listening to the patter of the asdic bouncing off the hull ever louder and faster, hearing it fade when the hostile destroyer was almost overhead, knowing that the depth charges would be sinking down towards them—all that horror might be more than nerve and fortitude could stand, just as an airman, high over Germany in the bitter cold, rocked by flak-bursts, blinded by the search-lights and hunted by the fighters, might suddenly decide that that kind of life was not for him. "LMF", or "Lack of moral fibre" was how the RAF described the condition; the USAAF, less harshly, called it "combat fatigue". Both in the bombers and the U-boats, the remedy was the same—to remove that man from duty just as rapidly as possible, before he infected the other members of the crew.

Nevertheless, the vast majority of men willingly endured the dangers, the squalor and the claustrophobic life, and they continued to do so again and again, on their missions to attack and be attacked by an enemy they seldom saw, sure in the belief that it was all for Germany, comforted by precious snapshots of their families and girl friends, encouraged by the knowledge that "Herr Kaleu" trusted them, that their crew-mates relied on them, and fully convinced that through their efforts this war would not end like the one their fathers fought, but in a famous victory for Germany.

Victory, however, was like a mirage in the desert, always just out of reach, and it seemed to recede further as the years went by. Losses mounted, more and more replacement crews were required and, with tens of thousands dying on the Russian Front, Dönitz no longer had the pick of Germany's young manhood for the U-boat arm. Given the choice, he would have chosen a high percentage of trained craftsmen, metal workers and machinists, men able to relate to a U-boat's working parts, to carry out repairs at sea and make replacements, but such artisans were also needed in the war industries and were hard to find.

Some of the new recruits were not well suited to

A sailor often wears a tattoo—/ For decoration, not as a taboo. / A confession of his every sin / Is also found on his martyred skin. / Among the anchors, ropes and sawfish, / Turtles, butterflies and starfish, / Reigns—as lovely as a pearl— / His once beloved, naked girl. / He holds her safe and strong and warm / On his lower left and hairy arm. / On the right one is etched a pair of hands intertwined, / Inscribed: Rosy, I'm yours with all the money you find. / Some other names of dames of late / Are all stricken out, including the date. / Yes, a deceived sailor never loses face; / His faithless girl is easy to erase. / A cross through her name, and another tattoo— / And Rose becomes Susy from Timbuktu.
—by Mechanic Mueller of *U-953*, from *Iron Coffins* by Herbert A. Werner

We Germans will never produce another Goethe, but we may produce another Caesar.
—Oswald Spengler, 1925

above left: At the desk of the navigator of *U-552* in April 1942. left: *Volunteer for the Navy*, a German Navy recruiting poster.

the underwater service—bare-faced boys, straight out of the Hitler youth, with little conception of what it meant to be at the mercy of the elements and no idea at all of how to conduct themselves in deadly combat. Nor was it any help to them that, from the beginning of 1944, most of the officers under training to command them were transfers from the Kriegsmarine's redundant surface ships, with little or no experience of submarines, while many of the men who should have become the next generation of U-boat commanders—those who had sailed with the early aces as 1st and 2nd Officers—were at the bottom of the sea.

Increasingly, also, the subordinate officers were rigid Party men; types who would not allow the crew's favourite jazz records to be played on the phonograph, because such music was non-Aryan or, worse still, American. Lectures from these officers, delivered during quiet times on patrol, tended to deal with such subjects as the way forward for National Socialism, which was not of much assistance when the next hunting Allied warship or aircraft came along. It did not take long for a recruit to realize the precarious nature of his situation: defeated soldiers could surrender or retreat, airmen had parachutes and stricken surface sailors had access to lifeboats, but a U-boat's liferaft held less than half the complement, and the personal escape-suit, out in the Atlantic, would be about as helpful as a clear understanding of the way forward for National Socialism.

When a group of men are being attacked, whether by bullet, high explosive or cold steel, the eternal optimist in each of them prompts him to believe that, although some of those around him will probably be killed, his guardian angel will somehow ensure that he survives. Since the time of bows and arrows, this euphoric belief has heartened nearly all fighting men—except those who went to war in submarines. They knew that when their craft was breached, deep down in the ocean, the fate of one would be the fate of all.

It costs me never a stab nor squirm / To tread by chance upon a worm. / "Aha, my little dear," I say, / "Your clan will pay me back one day."
—from *Thought for a Sunshiny Morning* by Dorothy Parker

...the periods at sea— cramped in mold-ridden, diesel-hammering, oxygen-lacking, urine-reeking, excrement-laden, food-rotting, salt-encrusted steel cockleshells, firing torpedoes in exultation, searching for convoys in frustration or receiving depth charges in stoic fear—these periods were the wholly admirable ones, regardless of who received the torpedoes or the depth charges, our side or theirs.
—Edward L. Beach, Captain US Navy (Ret.), from his foreword to *Iron Coffins* by Herbert A. Werner

left: Crewmen at their ease on board *U-103* in the summer of 1942.

17

THE NARROW DRUM

THE U-BOATS of the Kaiser's Navy in the World War I, and of Adolf Hitler's in the second, will always be the vessels best remembered for waging war at sea. They looked dangerous from the start, and their appearance did not lie. Their lethal reputation dated from the day in September 1914 when three heavy cruisers of the Royal Navy—then the greatest navy in the world—were torpedoed and sunk in a feat of arms that shocked the British public more than any Zeppelin bombing raid on London. This reputation was enhanced in the years that followed, when the great U-boat campaign against Britain's merchant fleet almost brought her people to the point of starvation.

The first known record of a working submarine (or more correctly a submersible) dates from 1620, in the otherwise undistinguished reign of King James I of England; if a contemporary account is to be believed, the monarch was persuaded by the Dutch inventor, Cornelius van Drebel, to take a trip in his oar-driven vessel on, and briefly under, the murky waters of the Thames. The first offensive action came in 1801, when a wooden, egg-shaped, one-man boat called the *Turtle,* designed by David Bushnell, had an unsuccessful crack at HMS *Eagle* in New York harbour during the American War of Independence. Equally unsuccessful was an attempt to sell the vessel to the Emperor Napoleon, who was currently engaged in a major sea campaign—a type of warfare of which he showed no more grasp than another European dictator, Adolf Hitler, in later years.

It was not until 1864, in the course of the American Civil War, that the thirty-foot Confederate submarine *H.L. Hunley* (the name of her builder), hand-cranked by a crew of eight, sank the 1,200-ton Federal sloop *Housatonic* off the South Carolina coast. Admittedly, her torpedo was fired on the surface, and she sank just moments later, but she had approached her target under water, and had shown for the first time what a submarine could do.

It was eleven years later, in 1875, that John P. Holland of New Jersey—the perfect picture of a 19th-century boffin, with his walrus moustache, rimless glasses, bowler hat, high wing collar and black frock coat—constructed a vessel that was to be the model for all the submarines of later years. The *Holland I*, with a crew of three, was powered by a steam engine when on the surface and by electric battery-driven motors when submerged; she was steered by a conventional rudder, and her depth was controlled by water ballast tanks; a little later, hydroplanes, like an aircraft's elevators, were mounted on each side of the bow to provide an element of longitudinal control.

The *Holland II* was developed in 1881 and was otherwise known as the *Fenian Ram*, in recognition of the Irish revolutionary party that, for reasons of its own, was backing the inventor—himself an Irish émigré. Thirty-one feet long, and displacing 19 tons, she was powered by an early model of the internal combustion engine and armed with a pneumatic 9-inch-bore cannon, which fired a 6-inch torpedo while under water. Strangely, the US Navy did not accept the *Holland II* for nearly twenty years, by which time five of the Holland submarines—the first that could be seriously regarded as weapons of war—were being built under contract for the Royal Navy by the British firm of Vickers. These led to the "D" class of submarines and in turn to the "E" class, which, with diesel engines, twin screws, saddle tanks, radio and guns, were comparatively reliable and formidable vessels. By 1914, the Royal Navy had a fleet of 74 submarines—the largest in the world—and when World War I began they were in action from the start.

In Germany, meanwhile, less progress had been made. It would be claimed later that a native son, Wilhelm Bauer, was really the true inventor of the submarine, but at the time his plans emerged neither the Navy nor the State gave him much encouragement. Admittedly, his first experimental launch, in 1851, was a failure and, furthermore, he was a soldier—a low-ranking soldier, at that—which

Amongst the manuscripts in the British Museum there is a quaint picture of a kind of a submarine barrel in which is sitting a crowned monarch. The barrel appears to have been transparent, and with the King, believed to be Alexander the Great, is shown a cockerel, and an animal which might conceivably be a cat; suspended from the roof of the submarine are three lamps with floating wicks. Above is a boat containing several people and the Queen, who appears to be holding a rope which is attached to the interior of the barrel.
—from *The Romance of The Submarine* by G. Gibbard Jackson

below: A Type IIB U-boat, the *U-23*. overleaf: Detail from *U-boats Meet in the Atlantic*, by Gris Freidel.

did little to commend him to the Kaiser's admirals. Bauer was obliged to seek a backer elsewhere, and it was more than fifty years later that a Spanish engineer, Raimondo d'Equevilley, who had studied submarine design in France, succeeded in persuading Friederich Krupp, the great German industrialist, to build what was to be the first of over two thousand German U-boats.

Neither d'Equevilley nor Krupp had an easy task: Grossadmiral Alfred von Tirpitz, founder and commander of the Kaiser's Navy, held the view that submarines might possibly be useful for coastal defence but for little else, and he saw it as his main task to build up a high seas battle fleet. It was not until December 1906 that the first *Unterseeboote*, *U-I* from Krupp-Germania, was commissioned. Soon after, however, more submarines were added to the strength, and the German engineers had the advantage that, coming on the scene later, they could skip the early experiments with steam power and gasoline for fuel and go straight to heavy oil (or paraffin). The result was that Germany's World War I U-boats were as good as or better than the Royal Navy's latest types. Even their periscopes, a field in which the British had originally excelled, were of superior quality.

By the end of World War I, all the combatant nations were building bigger, more powerful and better-armed submarines. Germany, indeed, had been planning to take the war to the coasts of America with a fleet of cruiser U-boats, each of 1,500 tons displacement, with a 150-millimetre gun, six 20-inch torpedoes, a surface speed of 17.5 knots and a speed of 8.1 knots submerged, and a crew of forty-six. This plan was postponed for twenty-four years by the Allied victory in November 1918, and the Treaty of Versailles banned Germany from building, buying or borrowing any kind of submarine. Britain, having suffered more from submarine attack than any other nation, was all for world-wide abolition, but when that advocacy met with no success she continued to develop her own fleet from the wartime "E" class to the "M" and "R" classes of the 1930s.

Work continued, meanwhile, on the development of countermeasures to the submarine, and this was an area in which the British had made a major breakthrough in 1917, when they devised a sonar detection apparatus. It was designated "asdic" after the Allied Submarine Detection Investigation Committee, under whose auspices it had originated. Asdic transmitted a narrow beam of sound waves

(which travel great distances through water, and at four times the speed at which they pass through air), to sweep the sea around the vessel. The sound waves produced an echo from any object in their path, the range of which could then be calculated from the time interval between the emission of the pulse and its return to the receiver.

The device, which the British made available to their French allies, gave a good guide as to the range and direction of a submerged U-boat up to a distance of about three miles, but gave only a rough indication as to depth. Asdic had other limitations: first, as the beam was directed at an angle, it was ineffective at close quarters; and, second, the operator had to be skilled enough to distinguish the echo of a U-boat from a host of responses caused by ocean debris, fish, plankton, rough water and even by sea layers of different temperatures.

In 1934, a year after Adolf Hitler's rise to power in Germany, the construction of U-boats was secretly resumed, and in March 1935 the Nazi regime openly repudiated the Treaty of Versailles. The prevailing mood among the wartime Western Allies was conciliatory, and there was a feeling in some circles that the terms of the Treaty might have been unduly harsh. The result was that, under the Anglo-German Naval Agreement, signed in London on 18th June 1935, Germany was permitted to rebuild the Kriegsmarine to a strength not exceeding 35 per cent of that of the Royal Navy, and 45 per cent in the case of submarines—a ratio later extended to 100 per cent. By 1935, Hitler's navy had six U-boats in commission, and more were on the way. Meanwhile the shadow of the swastika was steadily spreading beyond Germany's frontiers to loom over the Saar, the Rhineland, Austria and the Sudetenland; Poland, too, was threatened, and the purge of German Jewry began—a brutal, self-destructive programme that, with its subsequent exodus of intellectuals and scientists, was to cost the Third Reich dearly.

Over the years, the basic structure of the U-boat barely changed. The familiar long, tubular shape was formed by a steel outer casing containing the ballast and the "saddle" fuel tanks, with an inner pressure hull, three-quarters of an inch thick, which held the engines, the batteries, the control room, the torpedoes, the crew accommodation

The sea—this truth must be confessed—has no generosity. No display of manly qualities—courage, hardihood, endurance, faithfulness—has ever been known to touch its irresponsible consciousness of power.
—from *The Mirror of the Sea* by Joseph Conrad

The overbearing smells and the never-ending rocking made the men in the narrow drum dizzy and numb. Only the daily trim dive brought partial relief from the perpetual swaying.
—from *Iron Coffins* by Herbert A. Werner

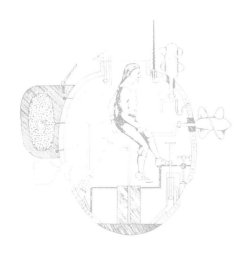

and the working areas. The ballast tanks could be either emptied under pressure from an air compressor when the boat was to surface or flooded with sea-water to submerge and control its depth; as the diesel fuel oil was consumed, sea-water could be let in through the bottom of the fuel tanks, both to reduce buoyancy when the boat was submerged and to prevent the tanks from collapsing under pressure when it went down deep. The boat was steered by conventional stern rudders, and the attitude was controlled by pairs of hydroplanes mounted fore and aft. The control room was amidships, with a hatch above it giving access to the conning tower and bridge.

The diesel engine-room was abaft the galley, with a closely-packed array of valves and switches, levers and turn-wheels, tubing, cranks and gauges, all gleaming coldly in the artificial light, amid a sound of clattering tappets and the thunder of combustion. The relatively silent electric motors were located in the stern, and their batteries' life was long enough to keep the boat in motion under water at an economic speed for about twelve hours; then, until the advent of the snorkel air pipes, the boat had to be surfaced to recharge the batteries with the diesels.

The main weapons were torpedoes, each one weighing a ton and a half, launched through tubes in the bows and in the stern. Mines could be carried in addition to, or in place of, torpedoes, and were

above: David Bushnell's *Turtle*. below: John Holland's first submarine. bottom: Holland's 1900 submarine prototype. below right: Inventor and designer John P. Holland.

discharged in the same way. Pairs of anti-aircraft Oerlikon machine guns were mounted on the after-deck, and the bigger ocean-going boats were also armed with 88- or 105-millimetre cannon forward of the conning tower.

Formidable as its record was, the U-boat had some intrinsic weaknesses as a fighting ship. The small surface area of the rudders and the fact that the screws were close together tended to make the turning circle wide; it had a comparatively low speed and limited defences, was highly vulnerable to counter-attack, and its range of action was restricted when submerged. Below fourteen metres—the length of the periscope—the U-boat was entirely blind, depending on sound-locating hydrophones for information as to where its enemy might be.

A further operational shortcoming was that the range of vision from the U-boat's bridge was much less than from a warship or, indeed, a merchantman. Over the years, some remarkable attempts were made to improve on this, one of which was to post a look-out in a bos'n's chair lashed to the top of the attack periscope, and another was to "fly" the look-out in an autogiro-like device, known as *Bachstelze*—"water stilt"—on a length of cable. Understandably, neither of these duties was eagerly sought after by U-boat crewmen.

The submarine's strengths lay in its fundamental seaworthiness, the low frontal silhouette which made it difficult to spot, its ability to achieve surprise—a basic principle of warfare—and in the fact that, alone among warships, it could hide. This last advantage, however, was offset to some extent by the extra weight of the electric motors and 50-ton batteries that were needed to propel it when it was under water. Since 1937 the German engineer, Professor Helmuth Walther, had been working on a method of producing steam for a turbine engine from a heated mix of hydrogen peroxide and oil but, despite pleas from Dönitz for a crash construction programme, it was some years before the Walther

O God assist our side: at least, avoid assisting the enemy and leave the rest to me.
—Prince Leopold of Anhalt-Dessau

left: *The U-boats Are Out!*, a 1917 poster by Hans Rudi Erdt.

engine came into production, and then only four were commissioned before VE-Day. Until then, two propulsion systems would always be required.

Although submarines were designed and intended to function under water, the fact is that for the first fifty years of their operational history they travelled and fought mostly on the surface; even when submerged, they seldom went deep—not much deeper, until the 1940s, than their own length. At that time, sonar detectors and depth charges were by no means as effective as they later became, and it was not until ship and air radars were developed further that the U-boats were

forced to dive more often and to stay down longer. Then, in the ding-dong battle between offensive and defensive technologies, the development of the snorkel made it possible to run the diesels at a depth where only the mastheads were detectable by radar or by eye.

The snorkel or "snort", was a Dutch invention originally designed as a simple wind scoop to provide a submarine with ventilation when it was submerged. A vessel so equipped was captured by the Germans when they invaded Holland, and they were quick to see its war potential. The ventilator tube was adapted to provide air to the

engines and a longer tube was added to serve as an exhaust, these tubes being raised and lowered, first by a winch and later by hydraulic pressure. Theoretically, with the snorkel as it was developed, a U-boat had no need to surface throughout the length of its patrol (one boat established a record by staying submerged for sixty-six days). In practice, however, there were certain problems. The spray from the exhaust tube could be seen for miles, tactically a drawback, and in a heavy swell the pressure of water was liable to block the outlet, causing an accumulation of carbon monoxide in the engine room that could put the stokers out of

action. Furthermore, if water covered the induction tube, a float valve closed it and the diesel engines sucked the air out of the boat, which meant no air for the crew.

The forces of drag act on submarines as they do on aircraft. On a U-boat they consisted of skin friction proportional to the hull's surface area and of form drag from all sorts of protuberances—cleats, air tubes, sailing lights, fittings for lifelines and towlines, torpedo tube shutters, exhausts, access and escape hatches, radio antennae and flood ports for the water ballast.

Submarines have a greater tendency to roll than

left: A U-boat under construction in 1940 at Germaniawerft GW-Kiel. below: Final fitting out of new U-boats at Krupp's Germania Shipyard. By the end of the war, the Krupp yard had built 168 of Germany's 1,099 submarines.

On 10th February (1942) we offered, unasked, twenty-four of our best-equipped anti-submarine trawlers and ten corvettes with their trained crews to the American Navy. These were welcomed by our Ally, and the first arrived in New York early in March. It was little enough, but the utmost we could spare. "Twas all she gave, Twas all she had to give."
—from *The Second World War: The Hinge of Fate* by Winston S. Churchill

above: A portion of the Blohm and Voss Shipyard facilities at Hamburg in 1995. B & V was one of several constructors of U-boats. right: An assembly yard at Bremen at the end of the Second World War.

surface vessels, and in a U-boat the primary weight distribution of fuel, weapons, stores and provisions was crucial to stability. A load of iron bars in the keel ensured that the centre of gravity was low, and no matter what forces were applied to it, either by nature or enemy action, no U-boat was ever known to have capsized. One of the Royal Navy's top U-boat killers, Captain Donald MacIntyre, once set the bows of HMS *Hesperus* against the beam of *U-223* and put on speed. The U-boat rolled over, righted itself and was back in Saint-Nazaire, only slightly damaged twelve days later.

On the surface, U-boats were more stable in the longitudinal plane than in the lateral, and vice versa when submerged. To maintain the trim—the boat's balance in the water—the levels in the trim tanks and the movement of the crew were rigidly controlled. The Chief Engineer even needed a daily report from the cook as to the disposition of the food on board. The slower a bicycle is ridden, the harder it is to balance, and a U-boat was just the same: a "stopped trim" was the most difficult to achieve, but if the Chief got it absolutely right, a pencil lying athwartships on the navigator's table would stay exactly where it had been placed.

In the same way as combat bomber aircraft were built around the bombs, guns and fuel tanks, U-boats were built around the torpedoes, engines, diesel tanks and batteries. Such space as remained was for the crew, their kit and their provisions. It was always at a premium: each officer and rating had his own small share of it for working and sleeping, and what was left over was used for storing food— carefully packed according to its shelf-life. Fresh food would be consumed first, followed by tinned and dried commodities. Huge smoked hams and strings of sausages—growing thicker with mildew by the day—hung over every deck; cans and packages were crammed into lockers intended for personal possessions. Men who liked eggs never needed to stint themselves: there were always enough to be eaten raw, boiled, fried or scrambled, with, before and after every meal. A U-boat man, in fact, was fed with more and better rations, albeit in less comfort, than any other member of the German armed forces in World War II.

At sea, on a *Feindfahrt* "operational patrol", the environment soon became noxious and noisome—damp with condensation, reeking of diesel oil, galley fumes, human waste and sweat. The crew slept in folding cots, fitted to the bulkheads and the walls and in the torpedo rooms, and there were only enough for half the complement to sleep at any time—the other half took over "hot bunks" when they came off watch. Water was reserved for drinking and cooking, and personal hygiene was never a priority.

Such were the vessels and the crews of the Kreigsmarine's U-boat arm on 3rd September 1939, when Grossadmiral Raeder signalled to his officers "Britain has declared war and we have no alternative. Total engagement. Die bravely." The British Admiralty's order to all Royal Navy ships carried the same import but without the gladiatorial undertone: "Commence hostilities at once with Germany."

THE LION

GROSSADMIRAL Karl Dönitz was and will probably remain the man most associated in world history with underwater warfare. Whenever the subject of the U-boat is discussed, it is a picture of Dönitz that comes immediately to mind—a tall, slim, narrow-shouldered figure, immaculately uniformed, with a pale, clean-shaven face, piercing eyes and sparse, fair hair brushed flat against the head.

He was born in a suburb of Berlin on 16th December 1891, the only son of a bourgeois Prussian family, and he joined the Imperial German Navy when he was eighteen years old. Like his father, he was intensely patriotic and quick to develop all the other traits expected of a German officer: unswerving loyalty, a strong sense of duty and a love of his vocation. His superiors were quick to recognize his possibilities and he was given his commission as a naval officer in due course.

For the first two years of World War I, Dönitz served as an air observer with a naval aviation squadron. He transferred to U-boats in 1916 and gained his first command on 1st March 1918. On 4th October, while it lay submerged off the coast of Sicily, his *UB-68* suffered a serious malfunction and involuntarily surfaced into the centre of a British convoy, whose escort promptly sank her. After ten months as a prisoner of war, most of it spent in an isolated Scottish camp, Dönitz was invalided home on the grounds of insanity, a condition that may or may not have been feigned. He remained convinced, despite his Mediterranean misadventure, of the U-boat's war potential and was sure that he knew how best to use it if the chance to do so should ever come again. His dream was of a massed pack, a *Rudel*, of U-boats, all working together under his command. Dönitz's love affair with "the wolfpack" had begun.

In the 1920s, when Germany was forbidden any kind of submarine by the Treaty of Versailles, it seemed a hopeless cause. Resuming normal duties as a naval officer, Dönitz had to content himself with preaching the U-boat gospel to anyone

and everyone in the Kriegsmarine and elsewhere who was prepared to listen, and his ardent advocacy eventually bore fruit. In 1935, when the outcome of the Anglo–German Naval Agreement was to let Germany resume submarine production (within certain limits), the first action of the Naval Commander-in-Chief, Grossadmiral Doctor Erich Raeder, was to send for a surprised but happy Kapitän zur See Dönitz, then in command of the cruiser *Emden*, and put him in charge of reconstructing Germany's U-boat service—the Ubootwaffe. This was clearly the right choice and, if Hitler and Raeder had shown as much faith in Dönitz's strategic foresight as they had in his ability, it is possible that World War II would have been yet more costly for the Allies than it was, that it would have lasted longer and that even victory might have been put in doubt.

Dönitz himself had no doubts at all and he started work on the planning stage of the *Rudeltaktik*. It was his belief that, in a future conflict, Germany's main target must be Britain's overseas supply lines, and that only his U-boats could fight a *guerre de course*—a war on trade. He knew from hard experience that the British had learned to meet the threat of the lone, predatory U-boat by moving ships in convoy, with warship protection; his new wolfpacks would elude the escort and destroy the convoy. For that, if it should come to war, he wanted 300 fast, medium-sized, highly manoeuvrable boats under his command. Of these, as he saw it, a hundred would be on station on the high seas, a hundred would be either on the way or sailing home, while the last hundred were re-equipping back at base.

The Type VII boat, about 750 tons, with five torpedo tubes and capable of operating in the Western Approaches and in the mid-Atlantic met his requirements. Building big U-cruisers, Dönitz counselled, or little 250-tonners that could only be effective in the North Sea or the Baltic, was a waste of effort and of money. But Hitler at that time was not preparing for war: his political advisers, and perhaps his stars, were telling him that neither the British nor the French would want to fight unless their global wealth were under threat. For a while, he was prepared to let Britannia rule the waves. His target date for a fleet of the sort of U-boats Dönitz wanted was 1945.

Dönitz's attitude towards Germany's new rulers was ambivalent. He was first and foremost a Navy man, with all that implied, but if the Nazis could avenge the humiliations of Versailles, and turn the tables on the British—the same *verdammt* British who had shamed and imprisoned him—and if they could lead the Fatherland to glory, then he would go along with them.

In 1938, while Neville Chamberlain, then the British Prime Minister, was flying home from Munich with a piece of paper bearing Hitler's signature and the belief that he had secured "peace in our time", Dönitz was ordering his officers to hold themselves in readiness for war. He dispatched twenty-five of his young commanders on "a fleet exercise" to patrol the waters from the Shetland Islands to the French Atlantic coast, to get a feel for what the future had in store. Three days later, he called them home to his secret HQ on the Baltic coast. "Next time", he said, "it might be the real thing, but don't wet your pants until the shooting starts."

When the shooting did start, Raeder wanted Dönitz, now designated *Befehlshaber der U-Boote,* or BdU (Commander-in-Chief for Submarines), to impose a blockade on all Britain's ports, and that, initially, was what Dönitz tried to do. But he soon convinced his chief that U-boats operating in British coastal waters were extremely vulnerable to land-based aircraft and that they should be cutting her lifelines out in the Atlantic, where the aircraft could not reach.

Of Dönitz's mixed bag of fifty-six U-boats (the Royal Navy's submarines numbered fifty-seven), forty-six were operational, but fewer than twenty-

five were ocean-going vessels—a far cry from his 300 convoy raiders—and for the first few months of 1940 there were seldom more than six on station at a time. The commanders and the crewmen tried not to disappoint the man they called "the Lion", and between January and the end of April they sank over 300,000 tons of merchant shipping. In the process, however, thirteen U-boats had gone down while others had been withdrawn for use in training schools, and Germany's ship-builders were unable to keep pace.

The French surrender that year gave Dönitz access to the harbours on the Channel and Bay of Biscay coasts, almost halving the time in transit to the Atlantic killing grounds. The effect was immediate. From June to October 1940—thereafter to be known in the U-boat arm as *die glückliche Zeit* "the happy time"—the raiders sank 274 merchant ships, with a total tonnage of 1,395,000, at a cost to themselves of only six boats. Although Britain's shipping losses were not so disastrous as in the darkest days of 1917, they still exceeded the available replacements.

In Germany, meanwhile, medals galore and tunes of glory greeted Dönitz's commanders when they returned to base and reinforcements for the happy few were on the way. In 1941 and 1942, latterly due to the efforts and the methods of the Minister of Munitions, Albert Speer, in producing prefabricated parts in dispersed factories, German industry began to turn out U-boats of the type Dönitz wanted at a faster rate: 91 were operational at the start of 1942, rising to 212 at the end of the year and 240 by April 1943. The fact that many U-boats built in 1941 were allocated numbers above 500 may have been a bluff—an early example of psychological warfare—or it may have simply meant that a particular contract had been cancelled, and that a block of numbers had disappeared.

Four hundred and thirty-two ships with a tonnage of over two million were sunk by the raiders in 1941, while aircraft, surface ships and

Dönitz...was a sour looking character, resembling Calvin Coolidge, but, like Coolidge, he had a sly sense of humor. They say he had an oil seascape hanging in his headquarters with nothing but white-caps visible in it. When visitors asked him what the picture represented, he replied, "The fleet passing in review in 1955." When they said, "But I don't see any ships." his answer was, "There are hundreds of them—submarines cruising in submerged formation."
—from *Twenty Million Tons Under The Sea*
by Rear Admiral Daniel V. Gallery, USN

Good communication is stimulating as black coffee, and just as hard to sleep after.
—from *Gift From The Sea*
by Anne Morrow Lindbergh

left: Grossadmiral Karl Dönitz.

minefields increased the toll to 1,299 ships and 4,328,558 tons. Dönitz was content with the U-boat arm's share of that; what irked him was that, although America was giving all possible aid to the British, Hitler had forbidden him to do anything about it. During the summer, there were several incidents in the Atlantic that clearly gave the lie to America's posture of neutrality, and these all came to a head on 1st September, when the Commander-in-Chief of the US Navy, Admiral Ernest J. King, ordered his warships to join the British and the Canadians in convoy escort duties within what had been established as the American safety zone. Three days later, the USN destroyer *Greer*, bound for Iceland, was warned by an RAF aircraft of a U-boat near at hand. After a three-hour chase by the destroyer, there was a brief and inconclusive exchange of weaponry—depth-charges from the destroyer and torpedoes from the U-boat. According to Dönitz, *Greer* had taken the offensive and *U-652* had been entitled to respond; the way President Roosevelt told it to his people, the U-boat Commander was guilty of piracy, and U-boats, just like rattlesnakes, had to be eradicated. Now America's kid-gloves were being peeled off.

In early December 1941, when America, long Britain's non-combatant friend, became her ally in the fight, Dönitz seized the chance to vent the fury he had up to then been forced to keep in check. His top commanders were operating in the Mediterranean or the South Atlantic, and his U-boats were scattered everywhere, but he mustered five long-range Type IXs, capable of staying on station for two weeks, and sixteen Type VIIs, which could be refuelled at sea. As for the commanders, here was an opportunity for some of his less celebrated Kapitänleutnants to join the aces' club. By the first week of January 1942 they were on their way to inflict upon America a defeat "compared with which Pearl Harbor was but a slap on the wrist", as Ladislas Farago, himself a wartime US Navy intelligence officer, described it in his fine

top: The uniform of Grossadmiral Dönitz at the Ubootarchiv in Altenbruch, above: The Admiral's pennant of Grossadmiral Dönitz, at the museum of the Hereford Regiment, right: WWI painting by G.S.Allfree, *Torpedoed Steamer off Longships, Devon.*

history of *The Tenth Fleet*.

Dönitz named the operation *Paukenschlag* ("beat on the kettledrum"), implying, with a certain grim humour, that he meant to begin the trans Atlantic battle with a bang. The drumbeat resounded through America, while the U-boats plied among the inshore traffic on the eastern coastline. "Bathers and sometimes entire coastal cities", the Admiral proclaimed, "are witnesses of the drama of war, whose visual climaxes are constituted by red aureoles of blazing tankers".

Well might Dönitz exult: by June 1942, the U-boats had ranged along the coast from New York harbour to the Straits of Florida and the Caribbean Sea, and they had sunk over 300 Allied vessels, including many tankers, in American coastal waters, as well as 90 more in seaways that the US forces were responsible for guarding. Many raiders needed to return to their bases to rearm rather than to refuel. "I am fearful", noted US Army General George C. Marshall, "that another month or two of this will so cripple our means of transport that we will be unable to bring sufficient men and planes to bear against the enemy in the critical theatres to exercise a determining influence on the war." With the U-boat arm responsible for 6,226,215 tons sunk in an overall Kriegsmarine total of 7,790,697, it was another "happy time" for them. As Churchill was to write: "The U-boat attack of 1942 was our worst evil."

In fact, the Atlantic convoys had gone virtually unmolested while *Paukenschlag* commanded Dönitz's attention. They had been able to sail direct for Britain on Great Circle routes—the shortest—with no evasive action, but the first six months of 1942 were hard times for the Allies. Rommel's Africa Corps had swept across Libya and was threatening the Nile; the Panzer divisions had surrounded Leningrad and were moving ever further east; Singapore, Britain's outpost in Malaya, had fallen, with heavy loss of life and many men inhumanely imprisoned, Japanese torpedo-bombers had sunk two British warships—the force commander's flagship *Prince of Wales* and the battle-cruiser *Repulse*—and in the Philippines American forces were making their last stand on Bataan.

Meanwhile, from his headquarters in a small chateau at Kernével, overlooking Lorient's inner harbour, Dönitz controlled his raiders by radio, constantly calling on his commanders to signal their positions and descriptions of the weather, and plotting each on the grid squares of a massive wall map, while marshalling them in response to convoy sightings, directing the attacks, and waiting impatiently for reports of sinkings and estimated tonnage. There was endless radio traffic, much of which was overheard and in due course deciphered by the British, but even if Dönitz had been aware of this, it is doubtful whether he could have denied himself the thrill of controlling the battle from a thousand miles away. The Lion roared from Lorient, and the wolfpacks made their kills. He called constantly for an unwavering pursuit, and a relentless attack, attack, attack. Korvettenkapitän Reinhardt Suhren was one who found his exhortations not only unnecessary but insulting, and at the customary post-patrol interview had the temerity to say so. The Admiral was momentarily astounded but recovered himself and grabbed Suhren by the neck, bent him over and, like an irate teacher with a naughty schoolboy, gave him a sound whacking on the rump.

It was Dönitz's firm conviction that a monthly average of 800,000 tons of shipping sunk would bring Britain to her knees. In fact, the existing rate in 1942 of almost 650,000 tons a month was having a crippling effect. It was just as well for the Allied cause that America was resourceful and strong enough, not only to withstand the disaster of *Paukenschlag*, but massively to multiply her contribution to the war in the Atlantic and beyond. Admiral King, putting aside, if only for the duration, his innate aversion to the British in general and the Royal Navy in particular, co-operated with them

completely in the ocean struggle. Although his feud with General "Hap" Arnold of the US Army Air Force was implacably sustained, any harmful effect it may have had on the conduct of the war was matched on the other side by the lack of harmony between Dönitz and the Luftwaffe chief, Reichsmarschall Hermann Göring. King, in fact, was to make a major contribution to the anti-submarine campaign by launching, and himself directing, the US Navy's Tenth Fleet. This, while being remarkable in that it had no ships, could call on other fleets for such vessels as it needed and had access to some of the best brains in America for research and planning.

The Allies' successful "Torch" landings on the coasts of Algeria and Morocco in November 1942 took the German Navy by surprise. "The German Intelligence Service under Admiral Wilhelm Canaris failed completely," Dönitz would complain in his memoirs, "just as it failed throughout the war to give the U-boat command one single piece of information about the enemy which was of the slightest use to us." The criticism was not entirely fair: Dönitz could have had assistance from the vast spy network of the Abwehr, but he had formed a low opinion of Canaris, also a submariner, when their paths had crossed in the early 1930s—and he had seen no reason to alter it since. He therefore preferred to rely on the radio intelligence service known as *B-Dienst*, which provided him with decoded intercepts of the Royal Navy's signals traffic.

Dönitz was energetic and charismatic, and he could be considerate: when the German radio revealed, in broadcasts that could be heard afloat, that the home-town of a U-boat crewman had been bombed, a signal from the Admiral would often follow, with some reassurance as to the welfare of his family. When necessary, he could be tough, thinking nothing of ordering a boat on patrol in the Azores, with a crew only kitted for the tropics, to re-deploy at once in the icy North Atlantic. He could also be duplicitous and had no scruples about concealing his losses from the

England expects that every man will do his duty.
—Admiral Nelson

To which Vice Admiral Collingwood in the *Royal Sovereign* muttered: "What is Nelson signalling about? We all know what to do."
—National Maritime Museum, Greenwich

We should lay up in peace what we shall need in war.
—Syrus

A cat pent up becomes a lion.
—Italian proverb

left: Young watch officer Karl Dönitz on the *U-39* in 1917.

R. M. S "LUSITANIA"   SATURDAY, JUNE 27, 1914

Menu

Hors d'œuvres—Variés
Canapé—Levasseur   Tartelettes—Moscovite
Chicken Okra   Crême Algerienne
Sea Bass—Egyptienne   Fried Filet of Flounder
Grenadins á la Florentine   Biscantins—St. Germain
Sirloin & Ribs of Beef
Haunch of Mutton—Boulangére   Turkey—Mephisto
York Ham & Spinach—Sherry Sauce
Green Peas   Rice   Fried Egg Plant
Boiled, Mashed & Persillées Potatoes
Asperges—Sauce Divine
Salade de Saison

Pouding Normande
Gâteau Vanille   Petits Fours   Rhubarb Tart
Gelée au Madere

Lemon & Coffee Ices

Dessert   Café

TO ORDER FROM THE GRILL (15 Minutes)
Sirloin Steaks   Spring Chicken   Mutton Chops

German public as well as from his own crews; or about accepting, and later publicizing, claims of sinkings by his commanders that he knew, or could have discovered, were exaggerated. He may have considered, though, that there was already quite enough bad news from the North African and Russian fronts, and from the bomb-battered cities of the Ruhr.

Strangely, it was not until the Casablanca conference in January 1943 that Churchill and Roosevelt gave the war against the U-boats top priority. Hitler was also turning more of his attention to the war at sea. He had been seriously displeased with the performance of the pocket battleship *Lutzow* and the heavy cruiser *Hipper* when, going against a Russian convoy off Norway on the last day of December 1942, they had been held off by five Royal Navy destroyers, and eventually driven off by two cruisers, without sinking a single ship. He gave orders for the big ships to be paid off as being of no further use to the Reich's war effort; he administered a dressing-down to Raeder and transferred him, after fifteen years as C.-in-C., to the less prestigious post of Naval Inspector General. At this, the Grand Admiral resigned, and on 30th January, Dönitz, again somewhat to his surprise, was appointed to succeed him in command. It was a big boost in prestige for the U-boat arm, but the older commanders regretted that the Lion had left them for a job among the *Schreibtisch Offizieren*—the paper pushers—and a lot of brass hats who sailed nothing but a desk. Furthermore, although Dönitz retained the title of Flag Officer U-boats, it meant that the immediate control of their operations passed to the faithful Chief of Staff, Rear Admiral Eberhardt Godt, who was as persistent as Dönitz in his use of the radio but lacked the master's touch.

As to the big ships, Hitler and Dönitz reached a compromise. The great battleships *Tirpitz* and *Scharnhorst*, with two pocket battleships and

IRISHMEN
AVENGE THE LUSITANIA

LUSITANIA

JOIN AN IRISH REGIMENT TO-DAY.

ISSUED BY THE CENTRAL COUNCIL FOR THE ORGANISATION OF RECRUITING IN IRELAND.   John Shuley & Co., Dublin.   Wt. P. 110—7,500   5/15

centre: A menu from the Cunard liner *Lusitania*, sunk on 7th May 1915 by torpedoes from *U-20* under the command of Walther Schwieger.

35

heavy cruisers, were retained on strength, while the older vessels were paid off and their complements transferred to the U-boat arm, which was in urgent need of reinforcements: seventeen new boats were being commissioned every month, and Dönitz was pressing Speer for many more than that.

The battle raged on, and heavy losses were incurred by both sides. By April 1943 over 400 U-boats were in service, and victory in the Atlantic was almost within Hitler's grasp. Then the Lion made what was probably his only tactical mistake, but it was a big one. He directed that the U-boats should sail on the surface to and from their battle stations and fight it out with aircraft if they were attacked. At the time, it may have seemed the right decision: the boats would make far better speed, and the eyes of the deck-watch might be more dependable than the Metox detector, which was failing to give warning of the Allies' latest airborne radar. By then, however, the Liberators, Sunderlands and Catalinas of the Allied maritime air commands were reaching further into the Atlantic, and carrier-borne aircraft, relieved from supporting the Allied campaign in North Africa, where Germany's forces had surrendered on 12th May, were available to protect the convoys all the way. Suddenly, the skies were full of hostile aircraft, and in the three months that followed, although fifty-seven Allied aircraft went down, it was at a cost of twenty-eight U-boats, with as many badly damaged.

Although it was not immediately apparent, the "happy times" were over: from then on, the tide of war in the Atlantic was always turning against Germany. This became evident in May, when forty-one U-boats and their crews went down, among them Peter Dönitz, the Admiral's younger son. Thirty-eight were lost in the Atlantic, six of them sunk by ships under the direction of the rapidly developing American Tenth Fleet. With hindsight, it can be seen that the decisive engagement was with convoy ONS5 in April 1943, when twelve merchant ships went down, but at a cost of seven U-boats (and others badly damaged) from the largest force that Dönitz could commit. It was a rate of loss that could not be sustained, and Admiral Godt, who had moved his headquarters into a Berlin hotel suite to be close to Dönitz, seriously thought of calling all the U-boats back to base. That, however, would have been an open admission of defeat, and besides there were only enough berths for 110 boats in the Biscay bunkers. A strategic redeployment seemed appropriate, and on 24th May 1943 the wolfpacks were withdrawn to the safer waters south-west of the Azores.

Now there were no action stories from the far Atlantic for the German press, no pictures of the heroes sailing in to port with their victory pennants flying. The U-boat arm had now assumed the Royal Navy's tradition of being "The Silent Service". The *Volkischer Beobachter*, the official organ of the Nazi Party, struck a plaintive note when it reported that Germany was fighting "American Generals, British archbishops and Soviet Jews, arm in arm".

Dönitz knew that great technical advances were just around the corner—the snorkel, new and better sonar, electronic compression of radio transmission, guide-by-wire torpedoes—and a new generation of fast, long-range U-boats, the Types XXI and XXIII. When they were available, he would return to the Atlantic and resume the fight. In the meantime, Dönitz appealed to the Führer, but he received short shrift: the Admiral's tentative suggestions that the Ubootwaffe might be used for landing storm troops on the coast of North Africa or for mining the main Egyptian ports were angrily rejected. "The Atlantic", spat an irate Hitler, "is Germany's first line of defence in the West." More calmly, he continued: "The enemy forces tied up by our U-boats are tremendous, even though the losses we inflict are no longer great. I cannot afford to release those forces by discontinuing our U-boat operations."

The U-boats sailed back into the ocean, but now to be hunted as often as they were the hunters, and

when the expected German technical advances came along the Allies had already developed the capacity to match them. The Atlantic battle was by no means over, but as each day passed and another great convoy reached a British port, it became more evident that Germany was losing it.

The days of glory were past, and so were the days when Dönitz would greet his commanders returning from patrol. Instead, they were called to make their reports at his headquarters (he changed HQ locations as the war went on). From the early days in Wilhelmshaven he had moved to the Maréchal Manoury Boulevard in Paris while the HQ at Kernéval was being prepared, then briefly back to Paris as Grossadmiral in January 1943, and then on to the Hotel am Steinplatz in an eastern suburb of Berlin; in April 1945, with the Russian Armies close at hand, he moved west to Holstein, north of Hamburg, and at last to Flensburg on the Danish border. There were no more dockside handshakes, no warm embraces, no pinning on of medals and no banquets. Nevertheless, the Lion was still idealized by the U-boat men, however rarely he was seen.

By the end of April 1945, chaos reigned in the higher echelons of the Third Reich. Believing, with some reason, that Göring planned a *coup d'état*, Hitler deprived him of his office and of the succession—indeed, if he could have found him, he would have had him shot. From the bunker under the Reich Chancellery in Berlin, where he was soon to die by his own hand, the Führer appointed Dönitz his heir as Head of State, and the Lion rose to the occasion. Duty to his country had always been his motivation, just as it had been to Nelson, England's greatest naval hero. Heinrich Himmler's prompt offer of his services as second-in-command was as rapidly declined, as was Joachim von Ribbentrop's bid for the post of Foreign Minister. Overturning other stones, Dönitz ordered the arrest of Josef Göbbels and Martin Bormann if they should happen to appear. One by one, the ghastly gang were put aside. "The last Führer", as a British journalist has

37

1116/3/9/39
FROM COMMANDER-IN-CHIEF U-BOATS STOP TO COMMANDING OFFICERS AFLOAT STOP BATTLE INSTRUCTIONS FOR THE U-BOAT ARM OF THE NAVY ARE NOW IN FORCE STOP TROOP SHIPS AND MERCHANT SHIPS CARRYING MILITARY EQUIPMENT TO BE ATTACKED IN ACCORDANCE WITH PRIZE REGULATIONS OF THE HAGUE CONVENTION STOP ENEMY CONVOYS TO BE ATTACKED WITHOUT WARNING ONLY ON CONDITION THAT ALL PASSENGER LINERS CARRYING PASSENGERS ARE ALLOWED TO PROCEED IN SAFETY STOP THESE VESSELS ARE IMMUNE FROM ATTACK EVEN IN CONVOY STOP DÖNITZ

So looks the pent-up lion o'er the wretch / And so he walks, insulting o'er his prey, And so he comes, to rend his limbs asunder.
—from *Henry VI*, Part III by William Shakespeare

described him, was in charge.

There was a brief hiatus while Dönitz insisted that the fight against the Western Allies must continue as long as they "hindered his resistance" to the Soviet advance, but on 8th May 1945 Winston Churchill was able to address the British people with these words: "At 2:41 a.m., at General Eisenhower's headquarters, General Jodl, the representative of the German High Command, and Grossadmiral Dönitz, the designated German head of state, signed the act of unconditional surrender of all German land, sea and air forces in Europe to the Allied Expeditionary Force, and simultaneously to the Soviet High Command."

At the post-war Nuremberg International Military Tribunal, when the four victor nations sat in judgement on the vanquished, Dönitz was charged with war crimes, conspiracy and crimes against peace, all of which he strongly denied. Dönitz agreed that his U-boats had been ready to fight in 1939, but when, he asked, had it been a crime for a soldier in peace time to prepare his troops for war? Surely that had been his duty to the German government and people. As for the horrors of the concentration camps, he had not known that they existed until the last days of the war. The Tribunal remained unconvinced. Dönitz was sentenced to ten years imprisonment—harsh punishment, but much less severe than that given to most of his fellow defendants. Speer got twenty years, Hess life, and apart from those who killed themselves, the rest were executed. There is little doubt that if Air Chief Marshal Harris, the British bomber chief—who also had won the fear and loathing of his enemies and the devotion of his crews—had been similarly arraigned by a victorious Germany, he would have faced a firing squad.

Dönitz was released from Spandau in 1956 and settled down to write his memoirs. He died in December 1980, never totally convinced that the British had broken the Enigma code in April 1941 and, for most of the last four years of war, had known as well as he did where his U-boats were.

Dönitz was proud, fond and protective of his young U-boat commanders. He had personally selected them, nurtured them and watched them through their training; to him they were always the bravest of the brave. Of German submariners he once wrote: "I was fascinated by that unique spirit of comradeship engendered by destiny and hardship shared in the community of a U-boat's crew, where every man's well-being was in the hands of all and where every single man was an indispensable part of the whole. Every submariner, I am sure, has experienced in his heart the glow of the open sea and the task entrusted to him, has felt himself to be as rich as a king and would change places with no man."

It has been suggested elsewhere in this book that similarities existed between the crews of Britain's heavy bombers and the crews of the U-boats— among them the long and lonely missions, the interdependence, the constant battle with the elements, the high prospect of death—and there were also likenesses between Dönitz and the C-in-C., RAF Bomber Command, Air Chief Marshal Harris. Both would always be uniquely identified with their respective war weapons—the U-boat and the bomber. Neither, strangely, had much personal experience of the sort of combat into which they sent their weapons and their crews. In his brief spell as a U-boat commander in 1918, the Lion sank one ship; between the two world wars "Bomber" Harris flew his sorties over the undefended north-west frontiers of India and the plains of Mesopotamia. Neither put his head above the parapet in the course of World War II, and in that respect they did not differ from any C.-in-C. since the Napoleonic wars. If Dönitz had led a *rudel* into the Atlantic, or Harris a mission to Berlin, it might have seemed a gallant action and raised their crews' morale; but if either had gone down, it might equally have been looked on as a foolish gesture, if not an absolute disaster. For their

crews, it was enough that they were the men they were, that they were totally committed, and that they never shrank from taking the hard option. They earned the regard and loyalty of many thousands, and ensured their places in the roll of great commanders.

The Admiral was probably not as inflexible as the Air Chief Marshal—some critics have described him as inclined to be erratic—and he was more of a romantic (it is hard to conceive of Harris writing the words quoted previously). But as force commanders, both had disagreements with their masters about the priority they should receive from industry and about the best way their forces should be used. Both men fought against diversions to objectives they saw as irrelevant. Both co-operated less with other military commanders than they might have done. Each believed that, given the means, he knew how to win the war—by inflicting enough damage on the enemy to render him defenceless. That neither quite succeeded was not for want of trying.

above left: Air Chief Marshal Sir Arthur Harris, whose bombers often attacked the pens and other U-boat targets. above: German cartoon implicating Churchill in the destruction of his own ship, the *Athenia*.

far left above: The house used by Admiral Dönitz as his BdU headquarters at Le Ter in Kernével. It faces the Keroman foreshore and the Lorient U-bunker structures. far left middle: The transverser at Lorient and one of the dry docks at Bordeaux. far left bottom: Quayside on the southern lock at Saint-Nazaire, the site of enthusiastic receptions for submarine crews on their return from patrol.

left: Admiral Dönitz is present to welcome the crew of *U-94* at Saint-Nazaire, 1st April 1942, on their return from operations.

1105/3/9/39
FROM NAVAL HIGH
COMMAND STOP
TO COMMANDERS-IN-
CHIEF AND
COMMANDERS AFLOAT
STOP
GREAT BRITAIN AND
FRANCE HAVE DECLARED
WAR ON GERMANY STOP
BATTLE STATIONS
IMMEDIATE IN
ACCORDANCE WITH
BATTLE INSTRUCTIONS
FOR THE NAVY ALREADY
PROMULGATED.

And pleas'd th' Almighty's orders to perform. / Rides in the whirlwind and directs the storm.
—from *The Campaign* by Joseph Addison

Pay attention to your enemies, for they are the first to discover your mistakes.
—Antisthenes

FOR THE infantryman the rifle, for the aeroplane the bomb, for the surface ship the big gun, and for the submarine the silent, sleek torpedo—the primary weapon at sea in both world wars. In the Royal Navy torpedoes were known as "fish", while in the Kriegsmarine they were called "eels" and the technicians who loaded and serviced them were known as the "mixers".

By the time World War I began, the torpedo had evolved through many stages of design development since the prototypes appeared in 1870. The early version had a diameter of 14 inches, an 18-pound charge and could run for 200 yards at six knots. Two years later, the English engineer Robert Whitehead quadrupled the charge, extended the range to 1,000 yards and installed a gyroscopic stabilizing mechanism. The developments continued through and after World War I, and by the time World War II began the torpedo had become a vessel in itself, launched by compressed air, with rudders and hydroplanes, and with its own guidance system and propulsive power, travelling at a speed of 40 knots.

Unlike the tank, the bomber and the armoured car, however, the torpedo had not been fully tried and tested in the forcing house of the Spanish Civil War, and some of the mechanisms had only been on trial in ideal conditions. Torpedoes had always been prone to misbehaviour, sometimes leaping in the water like a playful porpoise, sometimes running in a zig-zag like a hare across a field, and the torpedoes launched by U-boats in 1939 and the early 1940s were prone to other and more serious defects, as was shown in a report radioed to U-boat headquarters in Wilhelmshaven by Kapitänleutnant Günther Prien, patrolling off the coast of Norway in *U-47* on 16th April 1940:

"2242 hours, fired four torpedoes. Shortest range 750 yards, longest range 1,500 yards. Depth setting for torpedoes—12 and 15 feet. Ships stretched in a solid wall before me. Result nil. Enemy not alerted. Reloaded. Delivered second attack, on surface, after midnight. Fire control data

precise. Thorough inspection of all adjustments by Captain and First Lieutenant. Four torpedoes. Depth setting as for first attack. No success. One torpedo off course exploded against the cliff..."

There were many similar reports from commanders, both of premature explosions and of failures to explode at all. At the time, all the available U-boats were deployed along the western coast of Scandinavia in direct support of the Wehrmacht's "Operation Weser", the aim of which was to occupy Denmark and, subsequently, to drive the British Army out of Norway. In the face of the constant weapon failures, however, Dönitz decided to withdraw his boats (which had failed to sink a single ship), pending an investigation of the faults. It was a serious matter for the U-boat arm, but it was the British Army's withdrawal from Norway two months later that was to have a greater impact on the outcome of the war, for it caused the resignation of Prime Minister Neville Chamberlain and brought Winston Churchill into residence at No.10 Downing Street.

In essentials, the torpedoes of which Prien and his colleagues were complaining differed very little from those fired by their Admiral two decades before. They were 25-feet long, weighing 3,000 pounds, with an 800-pound high explosive charge that was detonated on impact by a firing pistol in the nose. A compressed air tank, located aft of the warhead, drove the engine, which in turn transmitted power through a gearbox in the stern to two contra-rotating propellers (the two-way rotation prevented the weapon's tendency to spin). The other components of the mechanism—the gyroscope and the balance chamber—lay between the engine and the gears.

The torpedoes could be launched at a range of three miles from the target, but most submarine commanders preferred to be within a mile before they fired. The lower limit, as then recommended in the manuals, was 300 metres—about a thousand feet. The target data—course, speed and range—as observed by the Commander or the 1st Officer,

EELS, HEDGEHOGS AND SQUIDS

Science is nothing but developed perception, interpreted intent, common sense rounded out, and minutely articulated.
—from *The Life of Reason* by George Santayana

left: In 1918 HMS *Terror* was torpedoed three times by U-boats, but it remained afloat and was brought safely to port by her crew.

On a submarine, more than on any other type of ship, each of the men who will live together for a year or so has a very high stake in the welfare and efficiency of this boat—his own life. Every man in a submarine knows that whatever future he has in life is bound to the fate of that submarine. If the boat dies, the odds are three to one he dies with her. He therefore not only does his own job to the very best of his ability, he checks to see that every other man does likewise. There is no such thing as an unimportant job and everybody knows that a single mistake by any one of them can be the end for the whole lot of them. Everybody resents any carelessness or inefficiency because the guilty party gambles with all their lives when he does anything that risks his own. A crew can be reconciled to a daring skipper who takes long chances and wins great glory for them to share, but they can't tolerate a stupid shipmate who doesn't pull his weight in the boat. After a submarine crew have made a couple of war cruises together, there is a bond between them that lasts for life. It bridges whatever gaps there may be in their background, education, and station in life, and makes them permanent members of an exclusive club who have shared certain experiences together that no other

whichever was at the master sight on the bridge, was passed through the TBT, (Torpedo Bearing Transmitter), integrated with the U-boat's own course and speed by a high-speed electronic calculator and automatically fed into the weapon's guidance system. There was no need to point the U-boat at the target—given all the targeting data, the torpedo steered itself.

The tubes were flooded on command, the aiming officer set the master sight's cross hairs on the target and the calculator's warning lights showed that it was doing the sums. The red lights went out, the white "ready" light came on and firing could commence at any time. The aiming officer kept the cross hairs on the target, called "Fire!", and pressed the button. The boat jolted slightly as the torpedo

left the tube, after which the boat's hydrophone operator, listening on the headphones, reported "torpedo running", and the appropriate trim tank, bow or stern was flooded to replace the weapon's weight and maintain the boat's trim. In the torpedo rooms the "mixers" stood by with chains and trolleys to reload the tubes on the aiming officer's command. Some minutes later, if the aim was true, they would hear the thump of the detonation, followed by the explosions and the awful sounds of metal rending as a ship went down. Like most of their fellow crewmen, they never saw their target.

A torpedo in its tube, like a bomb in the bomb-bay of an aircraft, was safe till it was armed, and, as with a bomb, the charge did not detonate until the spinner in the nose brought the firing pin in

line with the percussion cap. One of the problems experienced by Prien and his colleagues lay with the contact pistol, even the latest version of which had some inherent faults: not only was its operation peculiarly complicated, but the charge would fail to fire if the torpedo struck the target at an acute angle—which, on occasion, it was bound to do.

With magnetic detonation—using the target vessel's field of magnetism to activate the firing mechanism—the depth setting on the torpedo computer was less crucial than with impact detonation because an explosion underneath the hull was as effective as a hit below the water line, and usually enough to break a ship in two. The results still tended to be unpredictable, however, as the history of the British aircraft carrier *Ark*

Royal demonstrated. On 14th September 1939, in the North Atlantic, three magnetic torpedoes fired at her from *U-39* exploded prematurely, and her destroyer escort, guided by the towering plumes of water, found and sank the U-boat—the first to go down in World War II. Just over two years later, though, *Ark Royal* herself went down in the western Mediterranean off Gibraltar—sunk by a magnetic torpedo fired from the submarine *U-81*.

The records showed that U-boats using magnetic torpedoes in the Norway campaign had been no more successful than those employing contact detonation. The Torpedo Inspectorate, when questioned about this, produced an explanation— the magnets were being affected by the pull of the North Pole, or by the heavy loads of iron ore in

group in the world have shared. They may not all like each other, but for a certain period they pooled their lives together in a dangerous business and brought each other through it safely. They can therefore make allowances (ashore) for the failings of these shipmates which they wouldn't make for anyone else.
—from *Twenty Million Tons Under The Sea*
by Rear Admiral Daniel V. Gallery, USN

War is the science of destruction.
—John S.C. Abbott

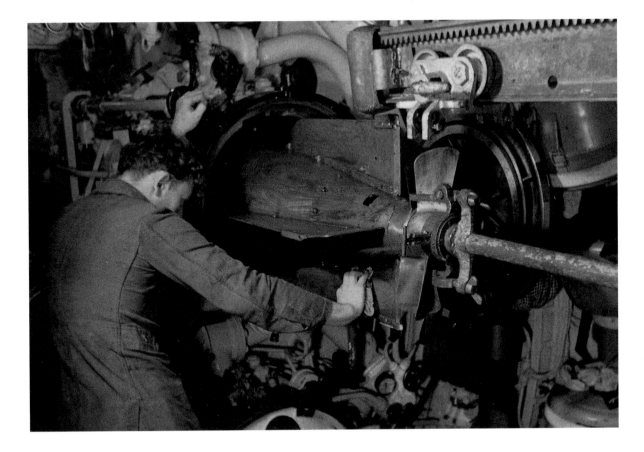

far left: Loading a torpedo aboard *U-124* in 1942. left: Loading an electric torpedo on *U-103* in May 1942.

below and right: Views of the forward torpedo room of *U-995*, on public display at Laboé near Kiel, Germany.

the Norwegian mountains, or possibly by both. Either of these influences may have had some effect, but the more likely cause of the magnetic pistol failures was the de-magnetizing process, either by "de-gaussing" or by "wiping", which had been applied to many British ships, as a protection against the magnetic mine. Whatever the reason, for a while, Dönitz ordered his Captains to use contact pistols.

A further problem lay in the faulty operation of the weapon's balance chamber, which controlled

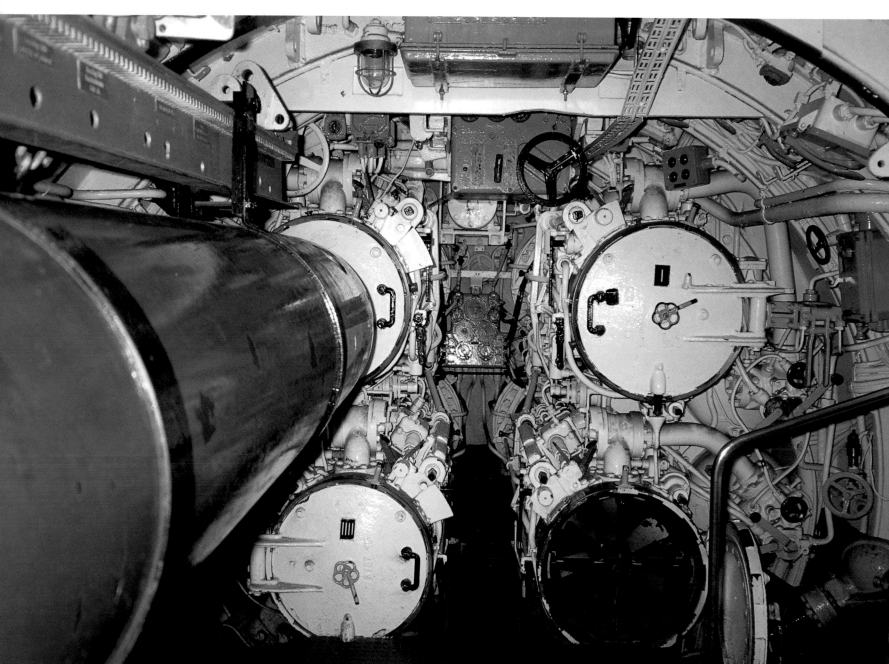

the running depth—a crucial factor—by means of a hydrostatic valve; the chamber was designed to be airtight but in fact was not, and torpedoes, which caused most damage when they hit the hull as low as possible, were tending either to hit too high, or to pass several feet below the keel and do no harm at all. It was a problem that was to stay with the U-boat arm for the next two years, and Dönitz, at the time, was heavily displeased. The blame, he decided, lay with the Torpedo Experimental Institute, whose staff, as he later wrote, "adopted an uncritical

findings led to the Court Martial of four senior members of the Institute's staff.

The next notable development was to replace the compressed air bottle with an electric motor, powered by a battery, and although the "E-torpedoes" needed much more maintenance than the air-driven "A-torpedoes", they had the advantage of not leaving a trail of luminescent bubbles in the water—which could alert the master of a merchant ship to take evasive action and also guide an escorting warship to its source.

...hit your enemy in the belly, and kick him when he is down, and boil his prisoners in oil—if you take any— and torture his women and children. Then people will keep clear of you...
—Admiral of the Fleet Lord Fisher, speaking at the Hague Peace Conference in 1899

attitude towards their own achievements", Gross-admiral Raeder, on being appraised of the situation, ordered an inquiry that concluded that over 34 per cent of the unsuccessful torpedo launches were due to weapon failure. These

In the torpedo section of the Kriegsmarine's U-boat manual, commanders were encouraged not to think in terms of economy when making an attack; if they found a worthwhile target, they should fire a salvo, even at close range, to make

above: *The Sinking of the SS Tekoa, Convoy HX229.* A painting by John Hamilton.

below: A Royal Navy destroyer in the Mediterranean Ocean in June 1942. right: A British corvette, HMS *Widgeon*, on convoy duty in the North Sea, readies depth-charges for firing.

sure of hitting it, and if the range were above a thousand yards, they should fire a "fan" of three or four. The experienced commanders used the methods that they found worked the best: some always fired a salvo, others were more frugal. The motto of Otto Kretschmer, the highest scoring ship-killer by any computation, was "One torpedo, one ship down".

Dönitz was still concerned about the series of failures that some commanders continued to report. His analysis showed that of 816 Allied ships attacked and hit by torpedoes between

January and June 1942, 40 per cent went down after one hit, while a further 38 per cent needed two or more, but that 22 per cent continued sailing after being hit by up to four. More modifications were urgently put in hand, and by the end of 1942 the depth control mechanism had been redesigned and a new magnetic pistol had been introduced that would also fire the charge on impact. By late August 1943, an acoustic guidance system had been developed for the T-5 torpedo, known as the "Gnat" to the Allies and *Zaunkönig* "Wren" to the U-boat force. This

Before a war, military science seems a real science...like astronomy. After a war it seems like astrology.
—Dame Rebecca West

below: US Navy men load hedgehog depth-charges. right: Mixers tend their missiles, which required frequent attention, adjustment and maintenance.

required less accuracy in determining the aiming angle because, once fired into the target area, the acoustic homer steered towards the loudest sound. The only problem was that, if the range happened to be incorrectly set, a Gnat might settle for the sound of its launcher's own propellers and come back like a boomerang. At least two U-boats were believed to have been sunk by their own returning Gnats. Acoustic torpedoes were ideal for air launch, though, and were used increasingly by Allied aircraft from 1943.

Late in 1942, the FAT (*Flachenabsuchender Apparat Torpedo*) and LUT (*Lagenuabhängiger*) became available. These were surface-running weapons programmed to travel for the whole estimated range before turning on to the target vessel's course, and then weaving to and fro until they either scored a hit or ran out of power. This

It takes some seconds for a depth charge to arch through the air and more seconds to sink through the water to its set depth, during which time a skillful sub skipper may maneuver out from under it. If he chooses to go down to say five hundred feet, he has quite a few seconds for his evasive maneuvering. If you miss him once he has that fifteen minutes reprieve during which he doesn't have to creep silently but can run at high speed while the ocean is reverberating and disturbed water conditions give your sonar phoney echoes.
—from *Twenty Million Tons Under The Sea* by Rear Admiral Daniel V.Gallery, USN

right: Depth-charges exploding over the contact spot indicated by the destroyer's submarine detecting apparatus.

development was meant to obviate the problems of accurate aiming in the rolling ocean waters, and to cut down the aiming time, since every moment on a steady course with the periscope in view was an invitation to the prowling escorts. Although justifiable tactically, this hit-or-miss idea would have been scorned by such marksmen as Kretschmer, Prien and Schepke. By then, however, they were no longer in the hunt.

Whether the torpedoes were powered, guided or detonated, they needed regular attention. Every few days the grease-smeared monsters were hauled out of their tubes by chains, pulleys, hoists and the muscles of the boat's mixers for all the systems to be checked—batteries or air bottles, engines and gearboxes, hydroplanes and rudders, gyroscopes and firing pins.

While the German scientists and engineers were striving to improve the U-boat arm's torpedoes, their opposite numbers in Britain, and later in America, were busily developing new counter-measures for use in their warships and maritime aircraft. Depth charges had always been the primary anti-submarine weapon and were to remain so (depth charges from ships or aircraft would account for 42.8 per cent of all U-boat sinkings), but those in use at the beginning of the war were just as antiquated as the early torpedoes of the U-boat arm, and the method of delivery— by being dropped through chutes in the warship's stern—had never been changed. However, the new ship-launched weapons, to be thrown instead of dropped, were designed to reach the target area before asdic contact was lost.

The first depth charge launcher to be used in action, in 1941, was "Hedgehog", a multi-barrelled mortar that fired a salvo of twenty-four "water bombs" in a circular pattern of about 130 feet in diameter ahead of the target on its estimated course. The mortar's mounting could be manually adjusted to allow for the rolling of the ship. The bombs, each with a 32-pound charge of Torpex, a

new explosive powerful enough to crack a U-boat's hull at a range of 25 feet, were designed to sink quickly and detonate on impact. Asdic contact was only broken if the weapon hit—at which point it hardly mattered. The Hedgehog's rate of kill steadily increased until, towards the end of 1944, it was touching 28 per cent—nearly five times better than the rate achieved by dropping weapons from the stern.

The next new weapon was "Squid", which came into service in 1943 as a complement to Hedgehog. Squid was a three-barrelled mortar that fired three full-sized depth charges, time-fused and aimed to explode in a triangular pattern round the target. Although Hedgehog's contact fuses meant that near-misses did not detonate and so caused no damage to the U-boat nor consternation to the crew, a hit with one of Squid's 300-pound explosive charges would destroy the U-boat, and a near miss would be enough to force it to the surface, where it could be dispatched by the warship's guns. Later, one of the mine-sweepers' proven instruments for combating acoustic mines was adapted to counter the acoustic torpedo. Containing a small but noisy engine, which sounded very much like a pneumatic drill, the "Foxer" was mounted in a dinghy towed astern, to attract the torpedo's sonar sensor.

So the ever-escalating, technological conflict between the weapons of attack and counter-attack at sea continued. The skill, the courage and the stamina of the opposing combatants would still play their part—man versus man, U-boat versus warship—but in the Atlantic Ocean they would not decide the outcome of the battle. That was to be waged between the offensive and defensive technological devices, sonar senders and receivers, radar searchers and detectors, magnetic guidance and demagnetizers, acoustic sensors and bafflers. It was a fight to be decided by men and women in design-rooms and factories, and here the Allies always held the upper hand.

SUPPLY LINES

BRITAIN never has been a self-supporting nation. She has always needed a volume of imports to survive, and in time of war it is the Royal Navy's task to keep the sea lanes open for the exchange of trade. In the 1930s, a third of Britain's food, including most of her meat, butter, cheese and wheat, came from overseas sources, while for home-grown crops, British farmers depended on imported fertilizers. Much of her steel and timber came from North America, and other essential materials were imported from all over the world: wool from Australasia, nitrates from South America, iron ore from Norway and Africa, cotton from the Americas, Egypt and India, rubber from Malaya, zinc and lead from North America and Australia, and oil from the USA, Persia and the Dutch West Indies. Three thousand merchant ships—freighters and tankers—were needed to carry the more than 4 million tons of resources that Britain needed every month.

In World War I the Kaiser's U-boats had brought the British people to the brink of starvation and would have achieved their aim but for the efforts of the Royal Navy, with massive assistance from the Commonwealth and Empire, and crucially from America. Dönitz knew all about that long campaign, and he was determined to do better the next time round. The primary target for the U-boat arm had to be not Britain's warships (although they would always be prime bonus targets) but the merchant shipping, without which her people could neither eat, run their industries nor continue fighting. Empty or laden, those ships must be sunk.

Although, at the start of World War II, the Royal Navy was not what it had been twenty years before—the policy of disarmament in the early 1930s had made sure of that—it still equalled the strength of any other Navy and was formidable enough to deter Hitler's admirals from contemplating the sort of set-piece battles that for all old sea-dogs were the only proper way to fight a

right: *Torpedoed Ship Sinking at Night*, by Julius Caesar Schmitz-Westerholt.

54

For the cause that lacks
assistance, / The wrong
that needs resistance,
For the future in the
distance, / And the good
that I can do.
—from *What I Live For*
by George Linnaeus Banks

below: This 18,000-ton
tanker, massively holed
amidships by a German
torpedo, awaits towing
back to port. Two of the
ship's crew died in the
torpedo explosion.

war. Grossadmiral Raeder was forced to agree that
a prime target for the Kriegsmarine had to be
British imports from wherever they might come.

Despite the havoc wrought on merchant
shipping by the U-boats during World War I, the
Royal Navy appeared to have forgotten most of
the lessons learned. The First Sea Lord, for example,
considered that the major threat would come from
German surface warships, and even his superior,
Winston Churchill, as First Lord of the Admiralty,
pronounced that the U-boats' early successes "need
not cause any undue despondency or alarm". The
requirement for organized convoys, with naval
protection, as practised by Britain since the 14th
century, and as demanded by Churchill himself in
the early days of World War I for ships carrying
troops and freight from Australasia to Europe,
was largely ignored when World War II began.

A slow ship sailing singly, like a heavy bomber
flying alone, once it was detected, was always
easy prey, whereas ships in convoy and bombers

in formation could offer some degree of mutual
protection and support. The speed of a convoy,
however, was limited to that of the slowest
vessel in it, and like large air formations convoys
were slow and awkward to manoeuvre in evasive
action. As the RAF knew, and the USAAF was to
learn, bomber formations needed fighter escorts
if they were to reach their targets and return. The
same was true of convoys—they needed warships
to protect them, or at least to discourage their
attackers. Statistics showed that, on the sea or in
the air, the straggling or stricken craft was always
more likely to be downed.

From the Royal Navy's point of view, convoy
escort was not the most sought-after of duties;
furthermore, there were not enough suitable
vessels or trained crews to undertake it. The fact
that air cover was almost non-existent until 1941
was not at all surprising, since the RAF, like the
Home Fleet, was crucially engaged in the defence
of Britain from German invasion—*Operation*

Sealion—and also in trying to take the war to Germany, albeit with bombers not far short of obsolescence. Furthermore, the degree of co-operation between the two services was not what it might have been, and it would be two long years before the Navy and the Air Force brought themselves fully to co-operate in protecting merchant shipping. In the early days, the Navy's Fleet Air Arm flew many gallant sorties against the German surface ships, taking off in single-engined Fairey Swordfish biplanes—"Stringbags" to their crews—from flight decks grafted onto freighters. Their navigation was by compass, rule and sextant, and their aircraft lacked the range, the armament and the effective search radar sets to hunt and fight the U-boats.

Meanwhile, the convoys formed and put bravely out to sea. The so-called "fast" convoys were by no means fast, and the slow convoys were very slow indeed. Sailing at an average nine knots, a "fast" convoy's passage time from North America to one of Britain's north-west ports was usually rather more than fifteen days; the slow ships took some four or five days more, and the convoys that formed at Freetown on the west coast of North Africa took about the same. Once France had fallen, Hitler's Axis partner Benito Mussolini began to threaten the Mediterranean, and shipping from the east had to take the long route round the Cape of Good Hope into the Atlantic— a passage time of many weeks.

Apart from the difficulties of mustering the vessels at the port of departure, of fuelling and provisioning them, of ensuring that they sailed together, stayed in position and maintained communication, the convoy system had certain other problems. One was that the installations at the ports of destination were intended for the regular day-by-day arrival of ships for berthing and unloading, not for the reception of thirty or forty vessels at a time. Another problem lay in the character of the merchant skippers, a sturdy and

(Action this day.)
Who has been responsible for starting this idea among the Americans that we should like their destroyer force to operate on their own side of the Atlantic rather than upon ours? Whoever has put this about has done great disservice, and should be immediately removed from all American contacts. I am in entire agreement with Mr. Stimson. May I ask that this should be accepted at once as a decision of policy, and that it should be referred, if necessary, to the Cabinet on Monday?
—Prime Minister to Foreign Secretary, First Lord, and First Sea Lord, 28.VI.41., from *The Second World War: The Grand Alliance* by Winston S. Churchill

Be near me when my light is low, / When the blood creeps, and the nerves prick, / And tingle; and the heart is sick, / And all the wheels of Being slow. / Be near me when I fade away, / To point the term of human strife, / And on the low dark verge of life / The twilight of eternal day. —from *Be Near Me When My Light Is Low* by Alfred, Lord Tennyson

Undoubtedly the greatest strains of the war at sea fell on the shoulders of the masters and deck officers of the tramp ships. Their charges were slow and manoeuvred like the lumbering barges they were. Station-keeping in convoy was for these men an unending ordeal. On a dark, moonless night it required nerves of steel and the eyes of a cat; in poor visibility or stormy

independent breed of men accustomed to taking orders only from their owners. In the opinion of one Royal Navy officer, who spoke from experience, the sinkings of merchant ships would have been far fewer if only their masters had done as they were told. None of this concerned the U-boat commanders: they simply wanted to find them, torpedo them, and leave them and their cargoes on the bottom of the sea; if their crews went down with them, *c'est la guerre*. In June 1940, food rationing in Britain was already strict, while with access to the produce of all the conquered nations—Poland, Czechoslovakia, Denmark, Sweden, Norway, Belgium, the Netherlands and France—Germany would never starve: the stubborn British in their islands surely would.

For their part, the British did not see it in that light. In the Submarine Tracking Room at the British Admiralty, U-boat positions, as indicated by whatever sources were available—radio intercepts, reports from secret agents in enemy bases, and air or sea sightings—were carefully plotted, and convoys were accordingly diverted or rerouted. In the early war years, however, there was always a shortage of escort ships and long-range aircraft, and the gap in mid-Atlantic between 15 and 20 degrees west, where the only defence against the U-boats was the lightweight armament of the cargo ships themselves, was known to the seamen of the Merchant Navy as "The Graveyard", and to the Ubootwaffe as "The Black Pit".

The life of the merchant seamen had never been an easy one. They were accustomed to its harshness and austerity, they had learned how to make a meal out of corned beef and hard tack, how to catch a few hours' sleep between their watches, if only on a locker top, and how to live with the impossibility of ever being dry. Now, however, they faced the threat of being torpedoed, mined and machine-gunned a thousand miles from land.

For them, the most fearful days of World War II came in the summer and autumn of 1940—the

period that came to be known in the U-boat arm as "die glückliche Zeit". It was at the height of this "happy time", on Saturday 5th October, that convoy SC7 sailed from Sydney, Cape Breton Island, Nova Scotia, en route for the Clyde. SC7 was the seventh of the slower convoys—those with a speed of just 6 or 7 knots—and it consisted of thirty-five ships, including three designed for sailing the Great Lakes of North America, along with various ancient vessels reclaimed from the scrap-yard. The majority were British, while some flew neutral flags—Swedish, Norwegian and Greek. Their cargoes were steel, timber, oil, grain, iron ore and sulphur, and they were escorted by a 1,000-ton Royal Navy sloop, HMS *Scarborough*, armed with depth-charges and two 4-inch guns. They would also be accompanied, for the first two days, by a seaplane and, less encouragingly, by an armed yacht. The convoy commodore was to be

...A NEEDLESS SINKING

Vice-Admiral Lachlan MacKinnon of the Royal Naval Reserve, who would fly his flag in the Liverpool-based cargo ship *Assyrian,* which, ironically, had been constructed in Hamburg at the start of World War I.

On the first day at sea one of the Lake ships turned back with mechanical problems, and it was replaced on the Sunday by *Shekatika,* a large British steamer that had failed to keep pace with a preceding convoy sailing out of Halifax. The formation, rectangular in shape and covering some five square miles of ocean, made up three five-ship columns, one headed by *Assyrian,* and five four-ship columns, with the longer columns stationed in the centre. The thinking was that, since U-boat attacks came mainly from abeam, the convoy's profile presented a minimal target and that the columns in the middle, where the tankers were stationed, were less likely to be attacked.

At dawn on the sixth day, in heavy seas, the remaining Lake steamers and two of the Greek ships were nowhere to be seen. Five days later, far off course to the south, and 27 miles astern, the Canadian Lake steamer *Trevisa* was torpedoed and sunk by the patrolling Kapitänleutnant Wilhelm Schultze in *U-124.* Six of *Trevisa*'s crew went down with her, and it was only by good fortune that the destroyer HMS *Keppel* came alongside in time to rescue the remainder.

On Thursday 17th October, twelve days into the voyage, the convoy had made its slow way past longitude 57 degrees north, and was just off the southern coast of Iceland, when it came within the sight of Korvettenkapitän Heinrich Bleichrodt on the bridge of *U-48.* Bleichrodt passed the news by short-wave radio to BdU in Lorient. Six other U-boats were within twelve hours sailing of that part of the Atlantic: *U-99* and *U-100,* respectively commanded by the aces Otto Kretschmer and Joachim Schepke, Heinrich Liebe's *U-38,* Karl-Heinz Mohle's *U-123,* Fritz Frauenheim's *U-101,* and *U-46,*

with Günther Prien's erstwhile 1st Lieutenant, Engelbert Endrass, in command. Dönitz then ordered them to form a barrier—a "stripe", as he called it—and to "mark time" across and forward of the convoy's course to the east of Rockall, the tiny island outcrop in the North Atlantic Drift.

Bleichrodt, however, decided not to wait. He launched his attack at four o'clock in the morning, and his aim was deadly: with three torpedoes, he destroyed the freighters *Corinthic* and *Scoresby,* and the 10,000-ton French tanker *Languedoc.* The escorting *Scarborough,* now joined by her sister sloop *Fowey* and the corvette *Bluebell* from Britain, picked up such survivors as they found.

Attacked by the escort, and later by a Sunderland flying boat, Bleichrodt lost contact and resumed his patrol, while his telegraphist signalled a report of the action back to BdU. Captain Dickinson, sailing in *Scarborough,* learned by radio of the Sunderland crew's sighting and showed fine fighting spirit, if not good judgement, by making his best speed to the position as reported. He hunted *U-48* for twenty-four hours, but he failed to find her, and was of no further help to convoy SC7.

In the early light of Friday 18th October, Liebe was the first of the reinforcements to arrive, and he was joined in the evening by the other five. Chancing on the straggling Greek grain ship *Aenos* while en route, Liebe had stopped her with a torpedo and sunk her by gunfire, but that was the limit of his success. The rest of the wolfpack, however, were in luck. They found the convoy, keeping good formation north of Rockall and making south-east for the Clyde. When Endrass in *U-46* launched the first attack at 8:15 p.m. Commander Robert Sherwood was on the bridge of *Bluebell.* "Suddenly", he said, "it was 'bang, bang, bang, and the place was lit up like Piccadilly Circus." For the rest of that night, despite every effort by the escort, now joined by the sloop *Leith* and the corvette *Heartsease,* the U-boats created havoc in a perfect textbook

weather it was an impossibility. They straggled, they romped and they veered, becoming the easiest of targets for the stalking U-boats. The men in the engine-room suffered the tortures of the damned, never knowing when a torpedo might tear through the thin plates of the hull, sending their ship plunging to the bottom before they had a chance to reach the first rung of the ladder to the deck. Burdened, as they so often were, with heavy bulk cargoes, the tramps sank like punctured tin cans filled with lead shot. For those who took to the lifeboats or rafts, the process of dying was more prolonged. Lacking protection from the sun and storms, and striving to exist on rations measured in ounces per day, many eventually succumbed to exposure, starvation, thirst or sheer mental exhaustion.
—from *The Merchant Navy Goes To War*
by Bernard Edwards

...this war of groping and drowning, of ambuscade and stratagem, of science and seamanship...
—Winston S. Churchill

demonstration of the wolfpack tactics—*die Rudeltaktik*—envisaged by their Admiral.

The light of a full moon shining through the drifts of cloud showed a dreadful panorama of floating wreckage, some of it still burning under palls of smoke, of flaming oil slicks, and of drifting lifeboats, some empty and others full of men. Among them the escort vessels speeded to and fro, the gunners firing "Snowflake" starshells, which, although they might illuminate a U-boat, provided the same service for the enemy and could temporarily blind the lookout on a merchantman at a crucial moment. Once, a torpedo, intended for a freighter, with its depth set for a vessel of that draft, passed directly below the keel of *Leith*, whose decks were taking on the appearance of a floating casualty station.

The Swedish vessel *Convallaria* with her load of pulp-wood was sunk by *U-46*'s torpedoes and she was followed to the bottom by the Cardiff ship *Beautus*, carrying steel and timber. Against the Commodore's instructions, the Dutch ship *Boekolo* slowed to save the crew of *Beautus* and, for her pains, was herself sunk. *Shekatika* went down, as did *Creekirk* with her crew and cargo of iron ore. Next to go was *Empire Miniver*, the biggest vessel in the convoy, then *Fiscus*, blown to pieces in an instant with her cargo of steel, followed quickly by the 1,500-ton Swedish *Gunborg*, laden with pulp-wood. Again defying the orders, but obeying their human instincts, the Greeks on *Niritos* turned about to pick up *Gunborg*'s crew. The latter, however, preferred the comparative safety of their lifeboats—a reaction not totally unknown in their condition. They waved the old Greek ship away, and on this occasion they were tragically right: barely ten minutes later, they heard the detonation and saw the vivid flames as *Niritos*, with her load of sulphur, met her end. When the U-boats broke off their first attack, nine ships of the convoy had gone down in two hours.

The next assault began at midnight, when the flagship *Assyrian* and half her complement went down, sunk by torpedoes from Frauenheim's *U-101*. Captain Kearon and Commodore MacKinnon were two of the survivors that were pulled out of the water by the crew of *Leith*. *Blairspey*, meanwhile, was torpedoed and abandoned. Downed in turn were the old *Empire Brigade*, the Dutch tramp *Soesterberg*, the Norwegian timber ship *Snefield*, the large British steamer *Sedgepool* and the Greek 10,000-ton *Thalia* with another precious load of steel. The *Clintonia*'s gun crew fought a brave but hopeless battle with two surfaced U-boats before they first torpedoed her and then blew her decks to pieces with their guns. When daylight broke on 19th October, only fifteen vessels of SC7 were afloat, and two of those were damaged. Throughout the action, just one U-boat was attacked by an escort, and this was without effect.

Leith raced around the shambles, her decks packed with men plucked from the sea, some injured, some dying, all soaked and frozen to the bone. The sloop's young surgeon Lieutenant strove, successfully, to save the life of Commodore MacKinnon, who at the age of fifty-seven had suffered greatly from the hours spent clinging to a pit-prop in the icy water.

Command of what was left of SC7 was passed by signal to Captain Thompson, the master of *Somerby*, and the convoy limped on towards the Clyde. Somehow, *Blairspey* had survived the impact of three torpedoes, and five days later the ocean rescue tug *Salvonia*, sailing out of Campbelltown, found her, reeling like a drunkard, and towed her into Gourock. *Leith* put into Liverpool, and her cargo of survivors were billeted all around the city, where German bombers made them welcome with an all-night raid. At least, the surviving officers would continue to be paid. Not so the seamen. It was one of the anomalies of Merchant Navy life that they came off the pay-roll when their ship was sunk.

Meanwhile, some 250 miles away, convoy HX79

Loose Talk can cost Lives

Keep it under your STETSON

Dawn was approaching, and with it the danger of aircraft patrols. From 500 yards he fired another torpedo at the *Invershannon*, which suddenly broke in half, and for a few minutes the crew of *U-99* were the sole witnesses of a sight reserved only for sailors in wartime. The two separate parts of the oil-tanker sank gently inwards and the two masts locked together at their tops, forming a great Gothic archway, under which black smoke and flames were thrust upwards from the bowels of a ship in its death-throes—a magnificent and terrifying scene bathed in pale moonlight. Around them the flurrying sea heaved and subsided, while over in the west a huge bank of black cloud gathered to emphasise the loneliness and vastness of the watery desert around them. Five minutes later the *Invershannon* gave its last, almost human, gasp of pain and was swallowed up by the waves.
—from *The Golden Horseshoe*
by Terence Robertson

far left: *Distant Escort*, by John Hamilton. top: Matchbook art. left: An illustration by Olaf Gulbransson.

63

out of Halifax was entering the Western Approaches with forty-nine cargo ships, two armed merchant cruisers, a Dutch submarine stationed in the centre of the convoy's six columns, and with the 5,000-ton *Loch Lomond* as a rescue boat. In the Western Approaches the escort was reinforced by the destroyers *Whitehall* and *Sturdy*, a mine-sweeper, four corvettes and three anti-sub

trawlers. So protected, HX79 sailed at a steady eight knots into the master sights of Dönitz's wolfpack.

Kretschmer and three more of SC7's attackers had expended their torpedoes and were sailing home, but Endrass's *U-46* and Schepke's *U-100* were still on station, as was Bleichrodt in *U-48* with one torpedo left, and these three were joined by Liebe in *U-38*. It was Günther Prien, however, on patrol

in *U-47*, who first identified HX79. Also low on torpedoes, he shadowed the convoy and called the others in. The wolfpack assembled during the evening of Saturday 19th October, and Liebe opened their attack at 9:45 p.m., sinking the British steamer *Matheran*. Two freighters went down, followed by the tanker *Shirak*, whose crew of thirty-seven were rescued by the trawler *Blackfly*. The tanker *Caprella* was sliced in two, and the motorship *Wandby*, hit by one of Prien's last torpedoes, was flooded in the engine room and had to be abandoned with her 1,500-ton cargo of pig-iron and timber.

The convoy Commodore ordered a dog-leg—forty degrees to starboard for thirty minutes and 80 degrees to port for a similar period to get back on course—but the wolfpack followed them relentlessly. Some engineers from the abandoned *Wandby* volunteered to board the stricken tanker *Sitala*, which had been holed by Schepke on the starboard side forward but was still afloat and apparently seaworthy. The engineers got steam up and set course for England, but when the wind freshened in the night her bow plates failed to take the strain, and the armed trawler *Angle* rushed up to save the men on board. A torpedo accounted for *Whitford Point* with her steel cargo of 8,000 tons; her Chief Officer, her bosun and a fireman were the sole survivors. With horrid irony, the last casualty, at 7:25 in the morning of 20th October, was the rescue ship *Loch Lomond*. Her crew, and the seamen they had saved, were taken aboard the minesweeper *Jason*.

The wolfpack had dealt with HX79 as efficiently and lethally as they and their companions had dealt with SC7. By the time they had finished, thirteen vessels of the convoy, including their rescue boat, were sunk. Of these, Endrass and Schepke each claimed three. The formidable escort had been no more successful than SC7's on the night before, and some reasons were clear. The senior naval officer had no experience of Atlantic escort duty, there had been no meeting of the captains before the operation, the corvettes were straight out of the shipyard and their crews were inexperienced. Designed for detection under water, their asdics received no echo from U-boats on the surface, and their depth charges had been ineffective. For inter-ship communication, they relied on loudhailers, signal lamps and flags. They had neither radar, nor any means of overhearing the U-boat's radio transmissions. As Commander Allen, Captain of HMS *Leith*, reported later: "With the present means available the difficulties of communications between the Senior Officer and other escorts... cannot be too highly stressed—and, as a corollary, the necessity for team work." Paul Lund and Harry Ludlam, in their *Night of the U-Boats*, put it even more strongly: "It was a story of inadequacy, unpreparedness and grim endurance on the part of the British, and cool, rewarding enterprise by the Germans..."

That same night, an outbound convoy from Britain came under attack, and another seven merchant ships went down. The destruction of thirty-eight vessels in the passage of three days and nights, at no cost to the U-boats, was a feat of arms that entirely justified Dönitz's belief in *die Rudeltaktik*. It also gave rise to an urgent reappraisal at the northern end of Whitehall of escort tactics, organization and equipment. For many of the complement of those ill-fated convoys that reappraisal came too late.

Firm in the belief, so often justified in wartime, that no news was good news, the Ministry of Information omitted to tell the British public about the convoy's slaughter, and the sole recognition of a host of gallant actions was the award of the Order of the British Empire to Captain Kearon, who commanded the *Assyrian*. But for the men who sailed the merchant ships, the inference was clear: every passage put their lives in the balance, and most of the weight was on the other side. "Unless

(Action this day.)
City of Calcutta, due Lock Ewe March 2, is reported to be going to Hull arriving March 9. This ship must on no account be sent to the East Coast. It contains 1700 machine guns, forty-four aeroplane engines, and no fewer than 14,000,000 cartridges. These cartridges are absolutely vital to the defence of Great Britain, which has been so largely confided by the Navy to the Army and the Air. That it should be proposed to send such a ship round to the East Coast, with all the additional risk, is abominable. I am sending a copy of this minute to the Minister of Transport. Another ship now of great importance is the *Euriades*, due Liverpool March 3. She has over 9,000,000 cartridges. I shall be glad to receive special reports as to what will be done about both these ships.
—Prime Minister to First Lord and First Sea Lord 28.11.41., from *The Second World War: The Grand Alliance* by Winston S. Churchill

...the gigantic world-wide trade of Britain, which...is never less than 2,000 ships at sea, and never less than 400 in the danger zones.
—Winston S. Churchill
9th September 1941

BITS OF CARELESS TALK ARE PIECED TOGETHER BY THE ENEMY

England

Convoy sails for tonight

right: The British Commander-in-Chief, Western Approaches, Admiral Sir Max Horton, in his office. above left and centre right: A U-boat editorial cartoon and a selection of wartime posters and images advising caution in all casual conversation, vigilance, confidence and patriotism.

we get protection", one seasoned master stated,"we shan't find men to crew our ships." The fact that matters never came to that must stand as a tribute to the spirit of the men who plied their trade upon the sea.

It was not until November 1942 that a firm British hand was laid on the progress of the Atlantic battle: Admiral Sir Max Horton was then assigned to the command of the Western Approaches (CINCWA in Allied terminology). Sir Max was an able, energetic officer, and in World War I he had been a successful submariner himself; indeed, his sinking of the German cruiser *Hela* on 13th September 1914 had been the first ever of an enemy warship by a Royal Navy submarine. He also happened to enjoy a game of golf, in which it was his habit to indulge himself on most afternoons. Having played his round at Hoylake, he would return to his office at Derby House in Liverpool, work late into the night, refreshed by a continuous supply of cordials, and reappear bright and early in the morning to resume his work. Much of that lay in out-guessing his opponent, Karl Dönitz, in a lethal game of bluff and double-bluff: "He will think I'll route the next convoy this way, so I'll send it that way" and "He will think that I think he'll route them this way, so we'll send the U-boats that way" and so on.

The dream of an anti-submarine Supremo, as voiced by Sir Philip Joubert when he was C.-in-C., Coastal Command, was never to be realized, but Sir Max's working relationship with Sir John Slessor, Sir Philip's successor, was the next best thing. It was Horton, perhaps more than anyone, who wove the strands of anti-submarine warfare into a coherent whole, and it was he, when Dönitz pulled his raiders out of the Atlantic at the end of May 1943 after the bitterest winter on record, who would send this measured signal to his ships: "The tide of the battle has been checked, if not turned. The enemy is showing signs of strain in the face of the heavy attacks by our sea and air forces."

FREE SPEECH
Doesn't mean
Careless TALK

THIS POSTER IS PUBLISHED BY THE HOUSE OF SEAGRAM AS PART OF ITS CONTRIBUTION TO THE NATIONAL VICTORY EFFORT

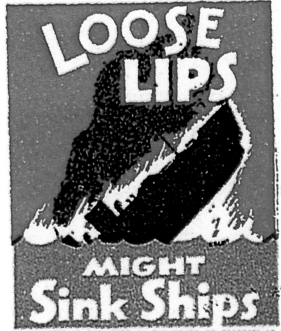

LOOSE LIPS MIGHT Sink Ships

THIS POSTER IS PUBLISHED BY THE HOUSE OF SEAGRAM AS PART OF ITS CONTRIBUTION TO THE NATIONAL VICTORY EFFORT

You are now a prize of the German Navy. You will set course for Bordeaux and on arrival inform the port authorities you have been captured by *U-99* and sent there to be taken as prize. Do you understand? Do not try to get away because I shall be following you below the surface. One deviation from your course and I shall torpedo you. Do you understand that?
—Otto Kretschmer, to the Estonian captain of a freighter stopped by the *U-99* on 11th July 1940.

"And then I got one this big."

THE
BRITISH NAVY
guards the freedom of us all

For us the Battle of the Atlantic was becoming a private war. If you were in it, you knew all about it. You knew how to keep watch on filthy nights, and how to go without sleep, how to bury the dead, and how to die without wasting anyone's time.
—from *The Cruel Sea* by Nicholas Montserrat

TYPE VIIC

OF THE MANY U-boat variations designed and built by German industry, the Types VII and IX, deriving from the *U-18* series of 1916, formed the majority of the Ubootwaffe, and although the larger Type IX had a longer range, carried more torpedoes and was better armed, it was the Type VIIC that bore the brunt of the campaign against the Western Allies' ocean-going shipping. As Edwin Hoyt has described it in *The U-Boat Wars*, it was "the most effective underwater fighting machine of all". More than six hundred of the boats were constructed and, in service, were responsible for nearly 60 per cent of all U-boat successes.

From the blunt shark-like bow to the tapered narrow stern, the Type VIIC measured 221 feet 6 inches; it had a draught of 15 feet, a beam (the widest part) of 20 feet 6 inches, a displacement of 769 tons. Expertly handled, it could be totally submerged in just over twenty seconds from the order "Dive!" The authorized safe diving depth for the early type VIICs was 100 metres (330 feet) and 25 metres deeper for the later models, of which ninety-two entered service.

In comparison, the 1,120-ton Type IXC was a little wider in the beam and 30 feet longer. It had a safety depth of 105 metres, but with its broader deck and larger conning tower, it took five or ten seconds longer than the Type VII to submerge, depending on the ocean conditions. Both the VIIs and the IXs could go twice as low as the official safety limits, and they frequently did so when that was the only way to avoid the depth charges.

The Type VIIC's best surface speed was just under 18 knots—slightly slower than the Type IX, and not as fast as a destroyer or a frigate, but fast enough to outrun the sloops and corvettes employed on convoy escort duties. Under water, carrying a hundred tons of water ballast to kill its built-in buoyancy, the top speed came down to 7.6 knots—just enough to keep up with the faster moving convoys and to overtake the slow ones.

With a normal fuel load of 113.5 tons of heavy diesel oil, running on the twin six-cylinder 1,400-horse-power M.A.N. engines at an economic cruising speed of 10 knots, the Type VIIC had a range of 9,700 nautical miles, but that was cut by a half if the top speed was sustained. Under water, running on the batteries at about two knots, the range was 180 nautical miles, reducing to 80 at a speed of four knots. The comparative figures for the Type IX were 11,000 nautical miles range sailing at its best speed, 16,000 at an economic speed, but a mere 134 at 4 knots when submerged.

The Type VIIC was equipped with four torpedo tubes in the bows and one in the stern, where the IX had two, and carried between eleven and fourteen "eels", depending on the task and the range of the patrol, while the Type IX could carry twenty-two. The deck armament varied from time to

right: At sea aboard *U-201*, December 1941. far right: Believed to be *U-96* in June 1941.

They go from strength to strength.
—Psalms. LXXXIV. 7

below: *U-995*, a Type VIIC boat displayed at Laboé near Kiel.

time, but the standard ordnance consisted of an 88-millimetre gun forward of the conning tower, with a 37-millimetre and two 20-millimetre anti-aircraft machine guns mounted on a platform (which the British called a "bandstand" and the Germans the "Winter Garden") abaft the bridge. This was an array of weaponry quite adequate for shooting up a merchant ship and for defence against a low-flying aircraft, but not for a gun-fight with a sloop or a

corvette, and certainly not with a destroyer.

Apart from those that were withdrawn from the high seas to serve in a training role, the Type VIICs were seldom used for any other purpose than offensive patrols, and their hunting grounds stretched from the North Atlantic to the Baltic, from the Mediterranean to the Arctic. With their greater fuel capacity, the Type IXs could and did range as far as the South Atlantic, the west coast of

Life, within doors, has few pleasanter prospects than a neatly arranged and well-provisioned breakfast-table.
—from *The House of the Seven Gables*
by Nathaniel Hawthorne

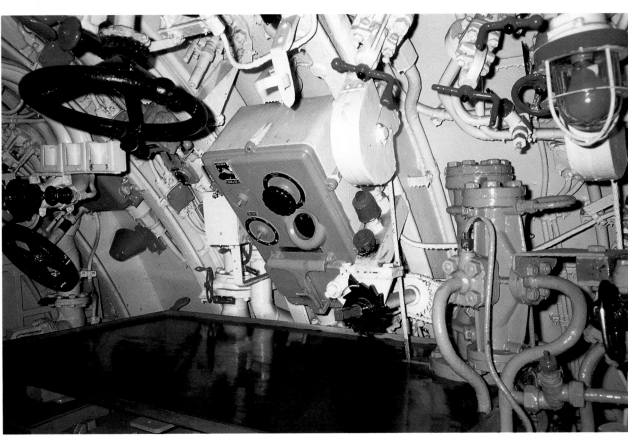

top: Engine-order telegraph of *U-995* at Laboé. above: Selector switch-box for the day-periscope, and the periscope sighting mechanism beneath the navigator's desk in the control room of *U-995*.

Africa and the Caribbean Sea. Variations of the Type IX, of which there were several, were used as supply vessels, carrying provisions, ammunition and fuel for transfer to the combat boats at sea. They were the "Milch Cows", which in theory could keep the Type VIICs on station for as long as there was a convoy to attack, or until Dönitz, in his mercy, called them back to base. In practice, the process of refuelling and rearming on the ocean was a lengthy and difficult operation, during which, for any Allied aircraft on the prowl, both the re-

fueller and the combat boat were sitting ducks.

The longer hull of the Type IXs meant that the crew environment was slightly less cramped than in the Type VIIs, and that was just as well: they could be at sea for up to fourteen weeks, as compared with the five or six for a VIIC's patrol. The Type IX's stern torpedo room was more spacious than the VII's, which gave more bed space for the crew, and a man could actually sit down in the lavatory, although his knees would still be up against the wall. Apart from these small expansions, there was

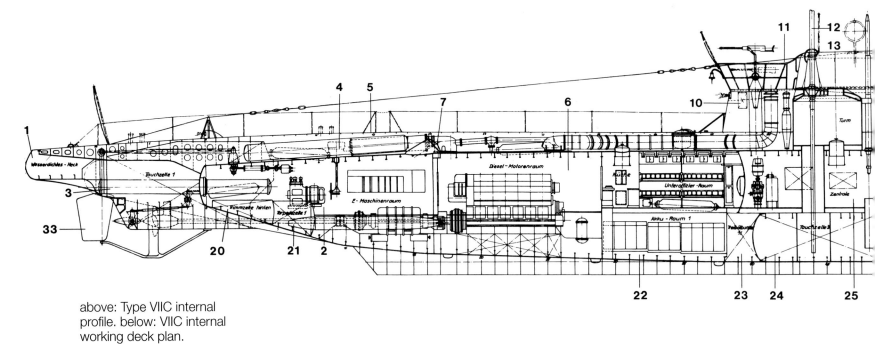

above: Type VIIC internal profile. below: VIIC internal working deck plan.

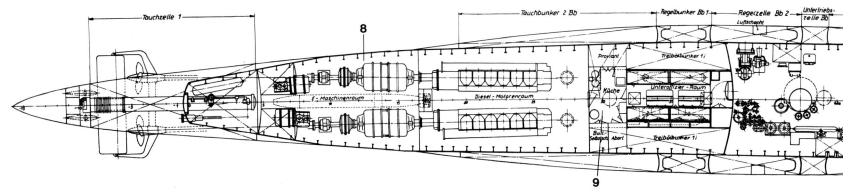

little difference below decks between the VII and the IX. Still not one cubic inch of space was wasted: foodstuffs hung everywhere, tables all folded, the back of every seat was a locker and every mess-room bench seat doubled as a bed.

The control room was amidships, with the conning tower above and the fuel and main water ballast tanks below. The control room was some 22 feet long and 20 feet across and was crammed with levers for the ballast tanks, buttons and spin-wheels that worked the hydroplanes and vents,

the Papenberg depth gauge, the Zeiss attack periscope, the navigator's table, the compasses (gyro and magnetic) and the electric steering gear. It was the boat's nerve centre, and the conning tower was its fighting heart. The conning tower contained the helm and the navigation (or sky) periscope, the Siemens-Schukert torpedo computer, linked to the bridge master sight and the gyro compass, and the fire interval calculator. The helmsman steered the boat from the tower or the control room, turning the rudders by the

Enemy submarines are to be called U-boats. The term "submarine" is to be reserved for Allied underwater vessels. U-boats are those dastardly villains who sink our ships, while submarines are those gallant and noble craft which sink theirs.
—Prime Minister Winston S. Churchill

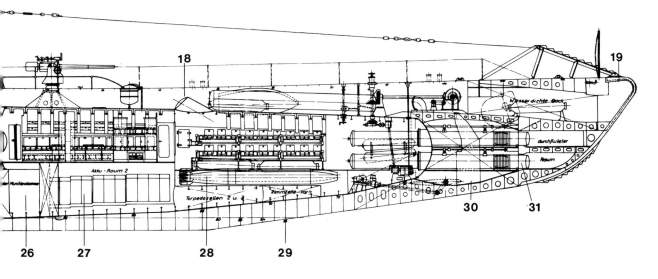

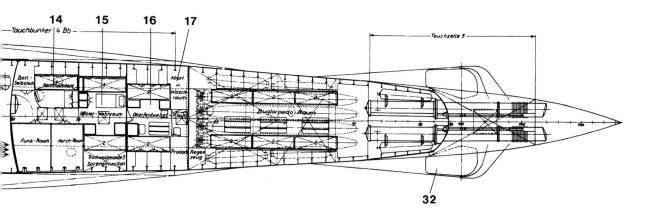

1. STERN CASING
2. STERN TORPEDO ROOM
3. STERN TORPEDO TUBE
4. RESERVE TORPEDO CONTAINER (WATERTIGHT)
5. UPPER DECK CASING
6. DIESEL ROOM
7. STERN TORPEDO LOADING HATCH
8. MOTOR ROOM
9. GALLEY
10. READY-USE AMMUNITION CONTAINER
11. WINTERGARDEN
12. ATTACK PERISCOPE
13. CONTROL ROOM-BRIDGE ACCESS HATCH
14. CAPTAIN'S CABIN
15. OFFICER'S WARDROOM
16. CHIEF RATES' QUARTERS
17. HEAD
18. FORWARD TORPEDO LOADING HATCH
19. BOW CASING
20. AFT TRIM TANK
21. TORPEDO COMPENSATING TANK
22. BATTERY ROOM 1
23. MAIN DIESEL FUEL TANK 1
24. MAIN DIVING TANK
25. CONTROL ROOM
26. MAGAZINES
27. BATTERY ROOM II
28. RESERVE TORPEDO STOWAGE
29. FORWARD TRIM TANK
30. ANCHOR WELL
31. TORPEDO TUBE III
32. FORWARD HYDROPLANE
33. STARBOARD RUDDER

below: *U-37* berthed at Lorient, February 1941. right: The distributor panel for high and low pressure on *U-995*.

below: The launching of a U-boat.

pressure of a button or, in emergency, by a hand steering system aft in the electric motor room. He always steered the vessel blind, changing and maintaining course by the compass, like a pilot flying in cloud.

The control room was separated by dished water-tight bulkheads from the fore and aft sections of the boat. Moving forward, a crewman would pass between the radio and sound rooms to starboard and the cubicle that served as the Commander's cabin to port. After this, he would pass through the officers' wardroom and quarters, past the twin lavatories or "heads" (one of which doubled as a supplementary food store for the first weeks of the patrol) and

through the petty officers' mess into the bow compartment—the "Bug-raum". Tiers of narrow cots on both sides of the boat, with hammocks slung between, provided the crew quarters, and they took their meals at a central folding table. The crewmen shared the compartment with the reserve torpedoes, which were chained above their bunks and stowed below the planks.

Moving aft of the control room, the prowling seaman would pass in turn through the combined utility room and petty officers' quarters, the galley, past the bulk of the one-ton air compressor, into the electric motor room and stern torpedo stowage, and through the diesel engine room to reach the stern tube.

The normal ship's company in a Type VIIC was forty-four: four commissioned officers—the Commander, with the 1st and 2nd Officers and the Chief Engineer—and ten Petty Officers responsible for the watches, the engine rooms, the electrics, the radio and control rooms, with a quartermaster, a coxswain, and a total of thirty seamen and technicians, including torpedo men, engine room artificers, electricians, telegraphists, control room hands and a cook. Cramped as they were, the crew had to find room for passengers— official observers, newly trained officers gaining combat experience, and the war correspondents— some of whom might be expected to pull their weight and take their share of the duties, while others only came aboard to get a glory story for the Propaganda Ministry.

The Type IXC's standard complement was ten officers and forty-four seamen, and while the Type VIIC's crew usually included a sailor with some first aid experience, the bigger boats carried a qualified doctor, seconded for duty with the U-boat arm. For emergency, the men were equipped with inflatable life-jackets, breathing tubes and masks, and a twenty-man rubber liferaft was carried in the outer hull forward of the bridge.

To give warning that an enemy radar was being

...her lines stood out...against the pale concrete wall above the low wharf. The casing was a bare metre clear of the oily surface. All the hatches were still open. The wooden planking which extended in one long forward sweep, flat and without sheer, to the bow; the conning-tower and cumbersome-looking anti-aircraft armament, the slightly inclined stern, the steel cable and green china insulators of the jumping wire which ran down forward and aft of the conning-tower. A picture of perfect simplicity: a VIIC U-boat, seaworthy as no other vessel afloat.
—from *Das Boot*
by Lothar-Günther Buchheim

The tiny, insignificant-looking submarines were being hurled high into the air by the mountainous swell, and then sent skidding down into the pits between waves, where they would be covered by raging seas before emerging high on the crest of another wave, where they hesitated for a brief second while the water drained off them before plunging downwards again. Often they just drove through the waves, which broke over them in foaming torrents.
—from *The Golden Horseshoe*
by Terence Robertson

below: The pumping station along the lock at Saint-Nazaire is the only WWII-era building remaining on the quay.
right: A watercolor of a U-boat lookout, by Rudolph Hausknecht.

beamed towards them, U-boats were equipped in 1942 with what, when compared with the rest of the gadgetry, was a surprisingly unsophisticated piece of kit, and one that a British serviceman would instantly have recognized as a "lash-up". It consisted of a bulky wooden frame in the shape of a cross holding a wire antenna that could pick up radar tranmission pulses at a range of about twenty miles. The frame was mounted on the deck abaft the bridge and manually rotated by the telegraphist on watch, who, if he could distinguish the pulses through the whistling and crackling sounds in his headphones, could read off the bearing of the searching enemy ship or aircraft.

One difficulty with the "Biscay Cross", as it

became known, was that, when the boat submerged, the whole apparatus had to be taken inboard through the conning tower; in a crash dive, it was liable to be trampled under foot by the watch as they came down the ladder in a rush. In the summer of 1942, it was superceded by "Metox", a legacy to Karl Dönitz from the fall of France, which received signals in the short-wave bands and was less of an encumbrance. Metox, however, became suspect when U-boats equipped with it were frequently jumped by Allied aircraft, which seemed to indicate that it acted as a homer. The suspicions were compounded by a captured British pilot who, on interrogation, said "we don't need radar to find

you chaps, we can pick you up on radio". That crafty airman lied. The increasing number of attacks were due to the Allies' latest centimetric radar, but the suspicion lingered on, and it was enough to persuade Dönitz, when he was appraised of it, to send an order to all U-boats at sea: "Switch it off." It did little for the crews' morale to learn, albeit incorrectly, that they had been beaming their position to the enemy for the last five months.

From 1943 many Type IX boats were equipped with the snorkel, and with a new radar detector in place of Metox, designated "W.Anz G1" and nicknamed *Wanze* or "Bedbug"; they had radio direction-finding (RDF) antennae, which were tactically useful but tended to extend the IX's dive-time even further, and "Aphrodite"—a towed hydrogen balloon filled with strips of aluminium "Chaff", like the Allied bombers' version "Window", to baffle the search radars.

"Bedbug" had automatic search control, which cut out the need for manual rotation, but the telegraphist had to be quick to recognize a signal and hold the antenna on the bearing; furthermore, neither it, nor its later variations, entirely fitted the bill. The German Navy's scientists were still firm in the belief that radar emissions in wavebands shorter than 20 centimetres would never give a good response, and they were only forced to reconsider in the early months of 1943, when pieces salvaged from a shot-down RAF bomber revealed that a radar on a waveband below 10 centimetres was in common use. Göring then demanded an all-out effort from the electronics experts to provide his night-fighters with a suitable detector, and in due course they came up with "Naxos", which was effective in the short-wave bands, if only at close range. For the U-boats, however, Naxos came too late. The underwater arm had fallen behind in the electronics battle, and by the time Naxos was installed, there were so many Allied planes in the skies that life had become one long sequence of alarm dives.

THROUGHOUT the Ubootwaffe's most successful years, the German newsreels, newspapers and journals regularly pictured U-boat commanders returning from the high seas, bearded, dressed in pea jackets, overalls and sea-boots, and with the white-covered caps which only they were authorized to wear, while, fluttering on a wire behind them, victory pennants showed how many Allied vessels they had sunk on patrol. Photographs showed them gravely standing at attention to shake the Admiral's hand, or, surrounded by their smiling crewmen, accepting the flowers, wine and kisses, and the plaudits of the crowd. Many U-boat commanders were *Oberleutnants*, a few were *Fregattenkapitäns* or higher, but the vast majority held the rank of *Kapitänleutnant*: "Herr Kaleu" to their crewmen, heroes to their Admiral and the German people.

One of Karl Dönitz's first actions when Grossadmiral Erich Raeder put him in charge of the U-boat force in 1936 was to turn the so-called Anti-Submarine School in Kiel into a training establishment for future U-boat officers. Three of those early students would become known as the bravest, ablest, most successful of all commanders in the Ubootwaffe. They were Joachim Schepke, Günther Prien and Otto Kretschmer.

Schepke was tall, fair and handsome, casual in manner, his cap always tilted at a rakish angle, popular with women and with no false modesty about his own attractions. Prien, known to his intimates as "Prüntje" and the oldest of the three, was born in Lübeck in 1908; the family had moved to Leipzig when his father, a judge, had quit the Prien home, and Günther's mother had brought him up alone. It may have been the contrast between the grime of the city and his early memories of the Baltic coast that turned his adolescent, lively thoughts towards the sea as a career. By 1939 he had spent nine years as a merchant seaman and six years in the Kriegsmarine. He was of medium build, dapper, something of a

loner and inclined to be impetuous, with a cheery smile and a stubborn nature.

The third of Dönitz's star pupils, Otto Kretschmer, was born in Lower Silesia. He showed an early interest in languages and science, and was sent to study these subjects in England, France and Italy before enlisting as a naval cadet in 1930. Although, when World War II began, he welcomed the excitement of taking his "canoe", the 250-ton *U-23*, on early probing missions into the northern British waters—these missions came to be known as "Kretschmer's Shetland Sorties"—he shared the view of many of his colleagues that the full weight of the Wehrmacht should have been directed to the East. "Silent Otto", as he came to be known, was hawk-nosed and slim, and an inveterate cigar smoker. He was intolerant of frailty but had a pleasant sense of fun. A mess-mate described him as a "friend of no one, popular with all". Probably, of the three future aces, Kretschmer had the keenest intellect and the strongest character.

In April 1940, Dönitz ordered Kretschmer to commission and command a new ocean-going Type VIIC, *U-99*, and this was the vessel in which he was to range the North Atlantic with deadly effect for the best part of a year. It was à la mode in the U-boat arm for the crew to paint—and constantly repaint—their own insignia on the conning tower (a fashion that would later be adopted by USAAF airmen on the noses of their bombers), and it happened that, while the crew of *U-99* were working-up in Kiel for their first patrol, one man noticed that a pair of horseshoes were hanging from the starboard anchor. Kretschmer accepted his 1st Officer's suggestion that this was an omen nobody could ignore. *U-99*'s new insignia would be a gilded horseshoe.

By the end of February 1941 Schepke and Kretschmer could each claim to have sunk more than 200,000 tons of Allied shipping. Indeed, most authorities credit Kretschmer with 50,000 tons more, including a destroyer and three armed

HERR KALEU

A life of action and danger moderates the dread of death. It not only gives us fortitude to bear pain, but teaches us at every step the precarious tenure on which we hold our present being.
—from *On The Fear of Death* by William Hazlitt

The feeble tremble before opinion, the foolish defy it, the wise judge it, the skillful direct it.
—Mme. Jeanne Roland

left: Korvettenkapitän and U-boat commander Günther Prien. His bold attack and sinking of the British battleship *Royal Oak* at Scapa Flow in October 1939 ranks among the most daring feats of the war.

merchantmen, and he was judged to be the best torpedo marksman in the German Navy. He did not subscribe to the official view that the best way to ensure a hit was to fire a "fan" of three or four and the proof of the pudding was that *U-99* seldom came home from a *feindfahrt* without a kill. Kretschmer's method was to shadow the convoy in daylight and approach at night—if in bright moonlight from the dark side, and on moonless nights from the windward side to ensure that the look-outs were facing into spray—and, then passing in between the escorts at periscope depth, to deliver his attacks from within the convoy columns.

Prien, meanwhile, had claimed over 150,000 tons. There had been an unhappy episode in an otherwise brilliant career when, in late June 1940, he torpedoed and sank, without warning, the 15,000-ton British liner *Arandora Star*, only to discover that most of the passengers were German and Italian civilians being shipped from Britain for internment in Canada.

The people of Germany, however, if not of Italy, would hear no word against their hero, for it was Prien who, shortly after midnight on 13th/14th October 1939, had crept into the Royal Navy's Orkney Islands anchorage, Scapa Flow, using all his sea-going experience to pass through the partially blocked Kirk Sound with the rising tide, and had found the 29,000-ton *Royal Oak*, flagship of the Home Fleet's 2nd Battle Squadron, lying at anchor. Three of his first salvo had missed, but the fourth struck home. Prien had moved away, reloaded, and fired four more torpedoes. Illuminated by the eerie glitter of Aurora Borealis, the great, old battleship went down in minutes. She was of World War I vintage and expendable, but the 833 officers and men who went down with her were not, and the disaster shook the Royal Navy and the British people, prompting a neutral merchant skipper justifiably to ask: "How can this happen, when the RAF have an airfield on the Orkneys?"

Prien's was a daring, skilful feat, and particularly significant for the Kriegsmarine and Germany

right: The white cap of
a U-boat commander,
displayed at the U-Boot-
Archiv in Altenbruch,
Germany. above:
A colour drawing of
Kapitänleutnant
Schuhart, also at the
U-Boot-Archiv.

because it was performed in the very anchorage where the Kaiser's high sea fleet had been sunk at the end of World War I—scuttled by their crews while the Allies pondered over their disposal. All aboard *U-47* knew that, and while they sailed south-east from the Orkneys homeward bound, the Executive Officer, Leutnant zur See Engelbert Endrass (himself a future ace), exercised his artistic talent by decorating the conning tower with a painting of a red, snorting bull—the bull, he explained, which had charged into the British Navy's haven and gored their famous battleship. It was an insignia later to be adopted by every boat in Prien's flotilla.

When *U-47* tied up at Wilhelmshaven three days later, brass bands played and a multitude cheered. Grossadmiral Raeder and Admiral Dönitz marched up the gangplank, buttons gleaming on their long dark greatcoats, and with their gold braided caps set squarely on their heads—Dönitz to embrace the Commander and pin an Iron Cross (second class) on every crewman's chest, Raeder to shake them by the hand. That afternoon, the crew were flown to Berlin in Hitler's private aircraft to be hailed by the citizens. Prien was driven through the Brandenburg Gate in an open limousine and received the sort of welcome reserved in the democracies for the heads of friendly, powerful states. In his private office in the Chancellery, Hitler conferred the Knight's Cross on the hero for what he called "the proudest deed that a German U-boat could possibly carry out".

Prien had done a lot more than sink a British battleship—he had made the Führer look upon the U-boat arm with a new regard and, incidentally, had won Karl Dönitz promotion to the rank of Vice Admiral. And, to the resoundingly titled Minister of Propaganda and Public Enlightenment, Doctor Josef Göbbels, the sinking of the *Royal Oak* was a gift. So overwhelming was the publicity given to the incident that Prien was embarrassed. "Damn it", he growled, "I am an officer, not a film star." It was a manly but ingenuous remark. He knew well enough that, since Scapa Flow, he was not and never would be just another German officer. The legend of the heroic, lone sea-wolf was born.

Prien, Schepke and Kretschmer soon became as popular with the German public as the RAF fighter pilots would be with the British when they fought the great air battles over south-east England in the months to come. Postcards depicting the young, smiling faces of the U-boat aces were on sale all over Europe, and stories of their exploits, sometimes with embellishments (Doctor Göbbels was not a man to underplay his hand) appeared throughout the land. Prien was persuaded to write the story of *My Road to Scapa Flow*, and Schepke produced a tract that was not so much a story as a recruiting pamphlet, chock full of Nazi propaganda, masquerading as an account of his exploits. Military bands played "The Kretschmer March" at every opportunity, but "Silent Otto" rejected all attempts to glorify him further (unlike Schepke and many of their fellow-officers, neither he nor Prien was a Party member) and waited until the war was over before putting pen to paper.

The day, however, of the ace U-boat commander, in the role of lone raider, was drawing to a close: Britain's overdue adoption of the escorted convoy brought about a change in U-boat tactics. Dönitz's dream was about to be fulfilled; the night of the wolfpack was at hand. In the early hours of 14th October 1940, Kretschmer's *U-99* sailed on her fourth Atlantic patrol as one of eight boats directed by headquarters to intercept a heavily escorted westbound convoy designated SC7. As has been described in the chapter *Supply Lines*, the raiders found their target after four days sailing, and launched a night-long series of attacks. Stealing to and fro among the freighters and the tankers, in between the escorts, *U-99* was never out of action or short of targets. Kretschmer's torpedoes and guns accounted for nine of the seventeen merchantmen sent to the bottom on that deadly

Oberleutnant Ottokar Paulssen was a short, stocky man in his early thirties; he had blond hair and blue, witty eyes that sparkled under the peak of his white Navy cap. The cap, which only the commander had the right to wear aboard, showed traces of verdigris on its brass ornaments. He wore a long jacket of light gray leather; its seams at the shoulders and pockets had been expertly hand-stitched with a heavy yarn. An artistic seaman's braid was fastened at his left epaulet with thread bleached almost white; and his feet, cased in large leather boots, stuck out beneath his wrinkled pants. In short, Paulssen fitted my picture of the ideal U-boat commander.
—from *Iron Coffins* by Herbert A. Werner

A hat is the difference between wearing clothes and wearing a costume; it's the difference between being dressed—and being dressed up; it's the difference between looking adequate and looking your best.
—Martha Sliter

top row from right: Kapitänleutnant Berger of *U-87*, Reinhardt Hardegen, Dietrich Borchert, bottom row: Karl Friedrich Merten, Robert Gysae, Helmut Rosenbaum, left: Werner Henke.

For what are the triuimphs of war, planned by ambition, executed by violence, and consummated by devastation? The means are the sacrifice of many, the end, the bloated aggrandizement of the few.
—from *Lacon*
by Charles Caleb Colton

We were now battling our way through the February storms, the severest of the winter. The sea boiled and foamed and leaped continually under the lash of gales that chased one another across the Atlantic from west to east. *U-230* struggled through gurgling whirlpools, up and down mountainous seas; she was pitched into the air by one towering wave and caught by another and buried under tons of water by still another. The cruel winds whipped across the wild surface at speeds up to 150 miles an hour, whistling in the highest treble and snarling in the lowest bass. When we were on watch, the wind punished us with driving snow, sleet, hail, and frozen spray. It beat against our rubber diver's suits, cut our faces like a razor, and threatened to tear away our eye masks; only the steel belts around our waists secured us to boat and life. Below, inside the bobbing steel cockleshell, the boat's violent up-and-down motion drove us to the floor-plates and hurled us straight up and threw us around like puppets. And yet we managed to survive the furious wind and water, and to arrive in our designated square in one piece.

—from *Iron Coffins*
by Herbert A. Werner

night. Back in Lorient four days later, Dönitz proudly described the achievement as "the greatest adventure story of the war". But Kretschmer found no great enjoyment in his later visit to Berlin, for neither meat nor alcohol was served in the Chancellery, and tobacco was strictly taboo.

The remarkable careers of Dönitz's three aces continued as members of the pack, and Hitler awarded the Knight's Cross of the Iron Cross with Oak Leaves to them all. By the end of March 1941, however, Prien and Schepke were dead and Kretschmer was a prisoner of war. Günther Prien had been on active service, with very little respite, since the first days of the war when, late on 6th March, he led a pack of six boats, including Kretschmer's *U-99*, in an attack on a westbound convoy out of Liverpool. In the next twenty-four hours four merchantmen were hit, and two of them went down, but the escort struck back with well-directed depth-charges. One U-boat was damaged and limped home to Lorient, another was abandoned and scuttled by the crew; Kretschmer, for once, saw discretion as the better part of valour, and left the scene of action, but Prien would not let the convoy go. He trailed it until the evening of 8th March and was closing on a target when a break in the showers he was using as a screen revealed his position to the destroyer HMS *Wolverine*. Prien crash-dived, but his boat was badly damaged; when he surfaced an hour later, *Wolverine* was waiting. The hero of Scapa Flow made his final dive. A doubt remains as to whether he was sent down by the Royal Navy or by another U-boat's maverick torpedo, but *U-47*, with its snorting bull insignia, exploded just below the surface and there were no survivors.

Ten days later, as Lieutenant Commander Peter Kemp put it in Purnell's *History of the Second World War*, "Schepke took too many liberties with a convoy escort". When *U-100*'s wake was spotted from the bridge of the destroyer *Walker*, Captain Donald Macintyre gave chase and dropped a pattern of depth charges at the point where Schepke had submerged. No result was evident, and *Walker* turned back to pick up the survivors from one of the four freighters the U-boats had torpedoed. Within half an hour, the newly installed radar on *Walker*'s sister ship HMS *Vanoc* had found *U-100*, lying on the surface while Schepke inspected the damage caused by the depth charges. The speeding destroyer then rammed the U-boat amidships, and her crew were either flung or jumped into the water. Schepke was standing on the bridge from which he had dealt out so much death and destruction when *Vanoc*'s bows sliced his legs off at the thigh; as the destroyer went astern to extricate herself, what remained of Schepke, arms flailing wildly, was torn free of the conning tower and flung into the sea. He, with *U-100* and forty-nine of her crew, disappeared beneath the swell. While *Walker* maintained an asdic sweep around her, *Vanoc* moved in to pick up the five survivors.

Within half an hour, the two destroyers had yet another asdic contact: they did not know it, but they had found the ace of aces. Their depth charges damaged the hull and both the propellers of Otto Kretschmer's *U-99* and drove him down to the dangerous depth of 700 feet. When at last he had to surface, the boat lay tilted heavily to starboard, with no torpedoes left and no means of manoeuvre, as helpless as a beached whale. On HMS *Walker*, Captain Macintyre now trained his guns on the superstructure, intending to force the crew to abandon ship and to take the U-boat in one piece. Kretschmer, however, was determined he should not: lighting a cigar in the shelter of the conning tower, he ordered his men to don their warmest clothes and to open all the hatches. The stern went under, and men on the afterdeck were washed into the sea.

Otto Kretschmer signalled Macintyre by lamp: "Captain to Captain, please pick up my men in the water who are drifting towards you. I am sinking." Gratefully, Kretschmer saw the destroyer's crew

left: *An Officer and Two Lookouts on the Bridge of a U-boat*, by Rudolph Hausknecht. overleaf: Kapitänleutnant Hessler, commander of *U-107*, is greeted enthusiastically at Lorient, 2nd July 1941.

right: Lieutenant
Commander Griffith
Bailey Coale's drawing
depicting the sinking of
the US destroyer
Reuben James. far right:
A U-boat captain's
binoculars, a part of the
U-Boot-Archiv collection
at Altenbruch, Germany.

prepare to lower a boat. Still the conning tower with the famous golden horseshoe stayed above the waves. An engineer asked Kretschmer's leave to go below and flood the ballast tanks. At last *U-99* went down, and the engineer went with her, as did two more of the crew. Treading water, the remainder held hands in an attempt to ensure no more were swept away. A scrambling net was lowered from *Walker*'s deck, and the U-boat men climbed aboard. Kretschmer, now exhausted, and with his sea-boots full of water, could only cling to the netting until his bosun came along to help.

Repeatedly, Lorient radioed *U-99* and *U-100*: "Report your position." The calls went unanswered

and unheard. Admiral Dönitz remembered telling Kretschmer that he had done more than enough, and that he should accept the offered post of Chief Instructor at the training school in Kiel; now, he bitterly regretted that he had not insisted.

The next day, Kretschmer stood on *Walker*'s bridge with Macintyre while the destroyer steamed around the convoy, which, as the British Captain pointed out, was moving in excellent formation and with no gaps in the columns. Macintyre smiled when he saw the German staring at the insignia on Walker's superstructure—an inverted horseshoe. "Yours was the wrong way up, Captain", he said, "and I'm afraid your luck ran out. By the way, you won't be needing those any more." So saying, he relieved Kretschmer of his Zeiss binoculars, which served the Royal Navy man well for four more years of war.

On 21st March *Walker* docked in Liverpool; Macintyre was piped ashore, and greeted on the quayside by Admiral Sir Percy Noble, the C.-in-C., Western Approaches, with his staff. The crew of *U-99* were handed over to the Army, and their Commander was taken to London for interrogation. He was interviewed there by Captain George Creasy RN, commanding the Admiralty's Anti-submarine Division, who later recorded his impressions in the book *The Golden Horseshoe*, Terence Robertson's excellent biography of Kretschmer: "He gave nothing away...I saw a young and obviously self-confident naval commander who bore himself, in the difficult circumstances of recent capture, with self-respect, modesty and courtesy."

Kretschmer was informed by his captors that he had been promoted to the rank of Lieutenant Commander with effect 1st March (as had Prien, posthumously), and that the Swords had been added to the Oak Leaves of his Knight's Cross. Men who had sailed with and learned from him, made their presence felt in the Atlantic long after he had been put "behind the wire". The last word about him must lie with his captor, Captain

'Good value, the Chief', was the Captain's verdict. 'Keeps a perfect depth when he has to. Does it by instinct. The new man'll never hold a candle to him—hasn't got the feel. Knowing your stuff isn't everything. You have to sense the boat's reactions and react yourself before anything happens. Experience plus instinct. Either you've got it or you haven't.'
—from *Das Boot*
by Lothar-Günther Buchheim

As *U-99* left the jetty, the dockyard superintendent and the staff came down to wave them good-bye. "She's a good ship, Captain," he cried out to Kretschmer on the conning-tower. "Treat her well and she'll sink the whole Royal Navy for you." "We will," shouted Kretschmer. "And I'll be seeing you when we take over Portsmouth dockyard."
—from *The Golden Horseshoe*
by Terence Robertson

At Dönitz's villa there was a constant two-way stream of radio traffic, information coming in from all over the Atlantic and orders going out to the boats at sea. I am amazed at some of the things for which U-boats in operational areas broke radio silence and reported to headquarters. Dönitz took a "calculated risk" on the incoming radio traffic and decided it was more important for him to get information than it was for his boats to keep radio silence at sea. Almost daily he arranged ocean rendezvous between U-boats to transfer spare parts for machinery, or to have homebound boats with extra fuel or torpedoes transfer the excess to boats remaining in the area, or to transfer a sick man to the nearest boat having a doctor aboard. He even held radio musters of his boats at times when he suspected trouble— ordering all boats to "report position and successes." It was by such a muster that he learned he had lost his three great aces, Prien, Schepke, and Kretschmer, early in March of 1941. When a boat in distress sent an SOS, Dönitz never failed to send nearby boats to her assistance. He was cold blooded in his orders that they were not to jeopardize their own safety by rescuing Allied survivors, but he took long

Macintyre: "Compared with his exuberant fellow aces he seemed a sinister figure. Out in the wastes of the North Atlantic he and *U-99* were indeed a sinister and deadly menace."

In the space of ten days, Dönitz had lost three of his best and bravest commanders, but while some of their contemporaries were pulled out of the firing line and either promoted or posted to staff or training duties, there was as yet no shortage of men ready to take their places in the ocean battle. There was Heinrich Bleichrodt, who had already

won his spurs in the Atlantic, Günther Hessler, whose fourteen kills in the course of one patrol would remain a Ubootwaffe record, and Erich Topp, whose thirty-nine sinkings in sixteen missions would include the destroyer *Reuben James*, the first US Navy warship to be downed. Among many others soon to make their names were Wolfgang Lüth, whose record of tonnage sunk would be second only to Kretschmer's, the expert marksman and maverick officer Werner Henke, Johannes Mohr, who was to sink the cruiser HMS *Dunedin* with a long-range shot on his second patrol in *U-124* and to add a corvette and thirty-two merchant ships to his tally, and Helmut Witte, who when he ran out of torpedoes and shells in *U-159* sent his men aboard a tanker to sink her with explosives and whose patrol of 135 days was the longest ever in the South Atlantic. In all, there were twelve U-boat commanders with authenticated claims of more than 150,000 tons of Allied shipping sunk.

In March 1943 Korvettenkapitän Werner Henke had defied a naval superstition by taking his new bride aboard *U-515* before setting out on what was to be his last patrol. It took the combined efforts of a US Navy Task Group and its aircraft to send the U-boat down. Henke and forty-three of his crewmen, many of them wounded, were taken aboard a destroyer and in due course sent to prisoner of war camps. During his incarceration, Henke got the impression, rightly or wrongly, that the Americans proposed to hand him over to the British, whom he believed would try and execute him for allegedly shelling survivors of the liner *Ceramic* in December 1942. Early in the evening of 15th June 1944 Henke completed his hour in the compound exercise yard, jumped the warning wire and sprinted for the outer barbed-wire fence. As he climbed, he looked the sentry on the guard tower in the eye, and the sentry shot him dead.

In September 1944 Kapitän zur See Lüth was appointed the Commandant of the Navy Training College in Flensburg, and it was to this

chances to save his own people...One effect of all this radio traffic was to make U-boat crews feel close to headquarters. They all knew that when and if they got in trouble an SOS to Dönitz would bring immediate help. This is important in an organization like a U-boat fleet, in which morale often affects results more than technical matters do.
—from *Twenty Million Tons Under The Sea*
by Rear Admiral Daniel V. Gallery, USN

I was astounded to see the food supply for eight weeks disappear between pipes and valves, ribs and machines, closets and ducts. Huge smoked hams were hung in the control room. Staples such as whipped cream, butter, coffee, and tea were locked up for distribution by the Captain. The fueling of *U-557* was accomplished on May 10. On May 12, we received loads of fresh vegetables, eggs, bread, and fresh water. We squeezed the crisp loaves into the last unoccupied crannies and filled three hammocks with the rest, letting them swing free in the bow and aft compartments.
—from *Iron Coffins*
by Herbert A. Werner

overleaf right: U-boat commander "Teddy" Suhren, among the most successful of the sub commanders.

Nothing is more difficult, and therefore more precious, than to be able to decide.
—Napoleon I

No more striking measure of the strong sense of security against U-boats which dominated all minds at Scapa Flow can be found than in the fact that, after one torpedo from the first volley had actually struck the *Royal Oak* none of the vigilant and experienced officers conceived that it could be a torpedo. The danger from the air was the one first apprehended, and large numbers of the crew took up their air-raid stations under the armour, and were thereby doomed, while at the same time the captain and admiral were examining the alternative possibilities of an internal explosion. It was in these conditions that the second volley of torpedoes was discharged. Thus the forfeit has been claimed, and we mourn the loss of eight hundred gallant officers and men, and of a ship which, although very old, was of undoubted military value.
—from " the loss of the HMS *Royal Oak*" speech by Winston S. Churchill 8th November 1939

IM NAMEN
DES DEUTSCHEN VOLKES
VERLEIHE ICH
DEM KAPITÄNLEUTNANT
GÜNTHER PRIEN
DAS EICHENLAUB
ZUM RITTERKREUZ
DES EISERNEN KREUZES

FÜHRERHAUPTQUARTIER
DEN 20. OKTOBER 1940

DER FÜHRER
UND OBERSTE BEFEHLSHABER
DER WEHRMACHT

If one U-boat skipper was consistently more successful than others working under similar conditions, the staff would study his methods to see how he differed from the rest. It usually turned out that the big factor in outstanding success was the personality of the skipper, and the staff couldn't do much about that.
—from *Twenty Million Tons Under The Sea*
by Rear Admiral Daniel V. Gallery, USN

The gentlemen got up to betimes to shoot, / Or hunt: the young, because they liked the sport / The first thing boys like after play and fruit; / The middle-aged, to make the day more short; / For ennui is a growth of English root, / Though nameless in our language:— we retort / The fact for words, and let the French translate / That awful yawn which sleep cannot abate.
—from *Don Juan, Canto XIII*
by George Gordon Lord Byron

far left: The awards of Günther Prien, including Submariner's badges, Knight's Cross to the Iron Cross, Oak Leaves to the Knight's Cross, Iron Cross 1st Class, Iron Cross 2nd Class and Four-Year Long-Service Medal. left: The citation for the Oak Leaves to the Knight's Cross.

below: Captain D.F.G. Macintyre RN, who captured Germany's greatest U-boat ace, Otto Kretschmer.

establishment that Karl Dönitz moved the remnants of the German government in the last days of the war. Despair and disillusionment were in the air, and everyone was tense. Just after midnight on 13th May 1945 a nervous young soldier on guard duty in the College grounds heard the sound of footsteps and shouted, "Who goes there?" He saw a dark figure, head down and moving nearer. He shouted again and fired what was meant to be a warning shot. The bullet hit the intruder in the forehead, and he fell. The guard had killed his Commandant, Wolfgang Lüth.

More fitting ends were those of Kapitänleutnants Engelbert Endrass, killed off the Azores on 21st December 1941, when the freighter he was shadowing at periscope depth executed a sudden turn and rammed *U-567*, and Johannes Mohr, who died in April 1943 when *U-124* was sunk by the escorts of Convoy OS45. Among others of the ace commanders, Günther Hessler, Helmut Witte and Erich Topp survived to make new lives in Germany, and Herbert Werner became an American citizen in 1957. Otto Kretschmer, on his release from imprisonment in 1947, returned to peace-time duties in the German Navy and, as Konteradmiral Kretschmer, became Chief of Staff to the NATO Forces, Baltic Approaches. Later, at a pleasant gathering in England, Captain Donald Macintyre shook his former prisoner's hand and then returned the fine Zeiss binoculars that he had "borrowed" in 1941.

Every one of these men, most of whom were in their late twenties or early thirties when the war began, was highly efficient in his deadly business, and in the long run that was all that mattered. It was Lüth, speaking in Weimar in 1943 on the subject of commanding men at sea, who said that a major factor in maintaining high morale was "the commander's success. Crews will always prefer the successful commander, even though he may be a fat-head, to the one who is consideration itself, but sinks no ships."

...he wanted to prove he could attack by night on the surface and carry out his personal principle of "one torpedo, one ship." Fans of torpedoes were, in his opinion, a waste of equipment and effort and allowed a U-boat commander to attack from a position of comparative safety in the hope of hitting something, instead of taking carefully calculated risks and by precision firing making every torpedo count. It was from this time that he became the first commander to attack convoys only by night and always on the surface. This attack was to set the pattern. At this stage of the war no other commanders followed Kretschmer's technique, considering it too dangerous, yet it was this method that led him to outstrip his colleagues in sinkings.
—from *The Golden Horseshoe*
by Terence Robertson

left: Korvettenkapitän Otto Kretschmer on the 'wintergarden' of his boat, *U-99*, June 1940.

THE PENS

AMONG THE RANGE of military benefits accruing to Germany in June 1940 from the capitulation of the Low Countries and the defeat of France was the acquisition of air and sea bases in western Europe. The ports which then became available to Dönitz on the French Atlantic coast, from Brest in the north to Bordeaux in the south, reduced the distance the U-boats had to travel to their killing grounds in the Atlantic by many hundreds of miles, enabling them to stay on station for ten days longer than when they were based in German ports. They also forced merchant shipping bound for Britain from the east to eschew the south coast docks at Portsmouth, Plymouth and Southampton and take the long route round, by the Bristol and St George's Channels, to the northwestern ports of Liverpool and Glasgow.

Dönitz was aware that the berths for his U-boats had to be protected from the RAF, and he persuaded Hitler of the need. He was referred to the Minister of Construction—Doctor Fritz Todt—who at once put his work force to the task. The OT (Organization Todt), with German engineers and construction experts, and with the assistance of conscripted and volunteer French technicians and labourers, began construction at a small fishing port near Lorient, which had initially been thought of only as a staging post—somewhere to rearm, refuel and resupply U-boats—while the flotilla headquarters and their administration remained back in Germany. By the time the OT had finished, Lorient was fully operational, with nineteen pens connected by channels to the harbour, massively protected and complete with all the necessary facilities—main services, fuel stores, the dry docks, workshops and accommodation, and defended by batteries of anti-aircraft guns. Known to the U-boat arm as "the ace of bases", Lorient was home to the 2nd and 10th Flotillas, each with an establishment of twenty-five U-boats, most of which were the long-range Type IXCs.

As the OT construction gangs steadily worked their way along the coast, building bunkers as they

It was April 4, 1944, when the train deposited me in the ancient, charming, but somewhat delapidated town of Brest. An old bus took me through town, crossed the drawbridge over the canal, coughed uphill, and continued westward on the familiar approach to the 1st U-boat Flotilla. I noticed a number of blimps floating gently over the harbor in the early morning breeze. They were a new defense measure installed to protect the U-boat bunker from low-level air attacks.
-from *Iron Coffins* by Herbert A. Werner

right: The U-boat shelters at La Pallice in 1996.

98

The (U.S.) VIII Bomber
Command flew its first
mission against the
submarine bases on 21st
October (1942), when it
dispatched ninety bombers
to attack the enemy base at
Lorient-Keroman. The
objective was a small fishing
port, situated about one and
one-half miles southwest of
Lorient on the Brest
peninsula, which the
Germans had developed as
a major submarine base.
Principal targets were the
U-boat shelters: twelve

far right: Brest peninsula
in 1944, right: U-boats in
a Biscay pen, below: The
Brest pens in 1945.

100

went, their progress was followed by incoming Type VIIC flotillas, also nominally twenty-five boats strong. The 3rd Flotilla moved into La Pallice, and later the 1st and 9th were based at Brest, and the 6th and 7th at Saint-Nazaire. Bordeaux housed the 12th Flotilla, with a miscellany of supply boats, mine-layers and refuellers, and a flotilla of some twenty-three submarines from the Italian Navy. Everywhere, the massive concrete structures dwarfed all other buildings in the harbors. Aircraft flying above them seldom saw a U-boat—only the flat, camouflaged roofs of the pens where they were hidden while being serviced, reprovisioned or repaired.

It was while the bunkers were still being built that the RAF's bombers should have struck, but at the crucial moment, and despite Churchill's statement in the House of Commons that "from being a powerful ally, France has been converted into an enemy", the Chiefs of Staff were persuaded by the Foreign Office that in all humanity the bombers could not strike the land and people of defeated France. Although many Frenchmen embraced the posture of the craven Vichy government, the majority of them did not, and no attacks were mounted until it was too late.

At last, as they had to be, London's qualms were put aside, and the Brittany bases—Brest, Lorient and Saint-Nazaire—came under air attack in 1942 and 1943. The results were disappointing. The RAF heavy bombers, committed to night attacks by their flimsy armament and to saturation bombing by their imperfect bombsights, effectively laid waste to a large amount of property in Lorient and Saint-Nazaire, but seldom hit the bunkers, and, when they did, they barely scratched their surfaces. The Fortresses and Liberators of the US Eighth Army Air Force based in Britain bombed with more precision, but their 2,000-pounders merely bounced off the concrete roofs and walls: the bombs then available to the RAF and the USAAF were not designed to penetrate the fifteen or twenty feet of reinforced concrete of which the

completed ones and a block of seven pens then under construction. Typical of their kind, these shelters had been built on dry land, then connected with the harbor by channels, and provided with heavily reinforced concrete roofs. Immediately adjacent to the pens stood lighter and smaller buildings believed at that time to contain workshops, transformers, oil storage, offices and other installations directly connected with the servicing of U-boats. Lorient had not been attacked by the RAF during 1942, nor had the British ever attacked the area of the submarine pens. In 1941 they had made thirty-three night raids, dropping 396.1 tons of bombs, mainly on the town itself. Although little major damage was done to the base itself, the (American) bombing made a great impression on both French and German opinion. For once, the French people appear to have compared an attack by U.S. forces favorably with those made by the British. They seem to have been greatly pleased with the whole affair, standing in the streets, watching and smiling and applauding the accuracy with which the Americans dropped bombs on the German installations. It was, they felt, too bad that Frenchmen had also to be killed, but the victims had asked for their fate in

overleaf: *U-boat in the Dock*, by Adolf Bock. below: *U-588* eases into a pen at Saint-Nazaire in March 1942. right: The arrival of a boat from patrol usually attracted spectators. below right: *U-106* and *U-124* in dry dock at Brest, 1941.

bunkers were constructed.

Brest, Lorient and Bordeaux were natural harbours, whereas Saint-Nazaire and La Pallice were not—they needed lock-gates to keep the water level constant—but even these were not attacked until the summer of 1943, when the Eighth Air Force made just one attack on each. Bordeaux was never seriously attacked at all. As for the bunkers, it

was not until 1944, when the RAF combined three 4,000-pound "cookies" into a single armour-piercing "Tallboy" bomb, that they could be hurt at all.

Of his Command's attacks in early 1943, Air Chief Marshal Harris was to write: "The most we could hope to do was to cause universal devastation round the [sub] pens and in the town...we could also give U-boat crews on shore a disturbed

accepting employment at the base for the sake of the high wages paid there. As for the Germans, they appear to have been taken completely by surprise. The alarm was not sounded, and the bombs had fallen before the antiaircraft guns went into action.
—from *The Army Air Forces in World War II*
by Wesley F. Craven and James L. Cate

Looking back over this first phase of the effort against the U-boat bases, leaders chiefly concerned with its prosecution could come to few conclusions regarding its effectiveness; it was easy enough to compile and quote certain operational data; ground reports and aerial reconnaissance pointed to certain specific effects. But it was much more difficult to determine whether any significant number of months of U-boat operations had been denied the enemy through these operations or to what extent, if any, the American bombing attacks had affected the number of U-boats operating in the Atlantic. Information gained since the cessation of hostilities indicates that the U-boats active in the Atlantic were steadily increasing in number during the period in question.
—from *The Army Air Forces in World War II*
by Wesley F. Craven and James L. Cate

right and below: From their bases in England, the heavy bombers of the US Eighth Army Air Force, and their Royal Air Force counterparts, made many attacks on the U-boat shelters of the French ports. The pens were a relatively short run from their bomber stations in the Midlands and East Anglia.

night, if they were foolish enough to stay in the area, but of course they were not. The Admiralty may or may not have thought that this would exert a worthwhile influence on the Battle of the Atlantic...though before we began on it I protested repeatedly against this hopeless misuse of air power...The only effect [the attacks] had was to delay the opening of the Battle of the Ruhr and the main bomber offensive against Germany by nearly two months."

The Biscay bases were well-defended by Luftwaffe fighters and by 88-millimetre anti-aircraft guns, and in the course of the attacks more than a hundred aircraft were shot down, over half of them USAAF bombers. Like Air Chief Marshal Harris, General Spaatz had doubts about the policy, and in October 1942 he wrote to General Arnold, his C.-in-C. in Washington: "Whether or not these operations will prove too costly for the results obtained remains to be seen. The concrete submarine pens are hard, maybe impossible nuts to crack." Accepting, however, that "the bombing of the surrounding installations should seriously handicap the effective use of the bases", he sent the bombers of the Eighth Air Force on eleven missions to the Brittany bases between October 1942 and April 1943, when both he and Air Chief Marshal Harris were given new priorities.

A French woman, who had been a girl of five at the time, would always remember vividly the shooting down of one particular bomber. "Our house in Brest was destroyed", she said, "but a few days earlier we had fled to a remote village. I was told that the 'Brestois' in their shelters prayed for the RAF pilots while the bombs were falling. On 13th August 1943, an aircraft fell in a field near our village. At the funeral of the crew, German soldiers forbade the locals to enter the church. The silence of what seemed to me a vast crowd was very impressive. When the proccession came out, the crowd moved forward but was stopped at the gate of the cemetery. I broke through the row of soldiers

and followed the procession. A German officer looked down at me but didn't say anything. Always, when we passed the cemetery, we prayed for the British pilots, and when spring came we brought bouquets of primroses."

Meanwhile, more than 600 Frenchmen were killed by the bombers, and their deaths were regretted in London and in Washington. Patriotic French men and women, however, members of the Resistance and the Maquis, shed few tears over those of their countrymen who died while willingly working for the Germans in the harbours.

By mid-1943, the streets of Saint-Nazaire and Lorient were full of rubble, trade and traffic were

BOMBS DROPPED BY TYPE OF TARGET / GERMANY / 17 August 1942–8 May 1945
U-BOAT AND E-BOAT BASES AND INDUSTRY
High Explosive=13856 tons
Incendiary=2874.9 tons
Fragmentation=164 tons
Total=16895 tons
DOCK AND PORT AREAS & FACILITIES
High Explosive=14582 tons
Incendiary=4801 tons
Fragmentation=46 tons
Total=19429 tons

BOMBS DROPPED BY TYPE OF TARGET / FRANCE 17 August 1942–8 May 1945
U-BOAT AND E-BOAT BASES AND INDUSTRY
High Explosive=2179 tons
Incendiary=0 tons
Fragmentation=0 tons
Total=2179 tons
DOCK AND PORT AREAS & FACILITIES
High Explosive=1475 tons
Incendiary=4 tons
Fragmentation=28 tons
Total=1507 tons

BOMBS DROPPED BY TYPE OF TARGET / NORWAY 17 August 1942–8 May 1945
U-BOAT BASES AND INDUSTRY
High Explosive=81 tons
Incendiary=0 tons
Fragmentation=0 tons
Total=81 tons

—from *Statistical Summary of Eighth Air Force Operations, European Theater, 17 August 1942 to 8 May 1945*

overleaf, top left: General James Doolittle who commanded the Eighth USAAF in Britain from 6th January 1944. remaining images: Typical activity on the American heavy bomber stations in WWII England, as photographed by the well-known *Vogue* fashion photographer Toni Frissell.

clockwise from top right: The pens at Bordeaux, and at La Pallice near La Rochelle, the massive turntable and the Dom bunkers of the Keroman foreland base at Lorient, the slipway and trolley for beaching U-boats at the Lorient Keroman pen complex, a modern submarine of the French Navy undergoing repairs in one of the Lorient pens, which has been pumped dry in 1996, modern metal sculpture being created in the rear service areas of the great U-bunker at the Bassin 2, Bordeaux, a rear service area entrance at the Bordeaux U-bunker and some of the U-beams that formed a bomb-trap roof structure, an open-air dry dock at the end of the Basin de Penhoët at the Saint-Nazaire U-boat base.

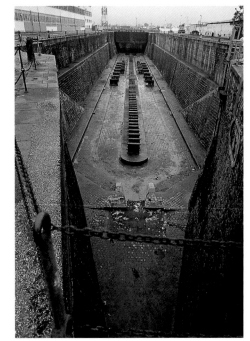

It was not until the end of 1943 that USAAF surveys of strategic bombing results tended to confirm doubts hitherto hesitantly expressed regarding the value of bombing submarine bases. By that time the submarine had been defeated in the first round of the battle of supply, and it had become apparent that attack from the air against the U-boat at sea had been the most effective single factor in reducing the German submarine fleet, and that bombing of bases had contributed relatively little in that direction. Grand Admiral Karl Dönitz, who, as one-time commander of the U-boat fleet, was in a unique position to know whereof he spoke, later confirmed this opinion in an interview with Allied intelligence officers after his capture in 1945. Not only were the pens themselves impervious to anything but the heaviest type of bomb, he asserted, but they housed virtually all necessary repair and maintenance facilities. Bombing of surrounding installations did not therefore seriously affect the rate of turn-around. What slowed turn-around most effectively, he claimed, was the necessity for repairing the damage done to hull structure by aerial-bomb and depth-charge attacks delivered at sea.
—from *The Army Air Forces In World War II*
by Wesley F. Craven
and James L. Cate

Despite the most rigid checks by the Gestapo on the French shipyard workers, underground agents actually wormed their way into the yards where the U-boats were readied for their next cruises. These seeming collaborators, ostensibly working for the Germans, slipped little bags of sugar into the lubricating oil tanks of U-boats. The sugar dissolved into the oil and those U-boats came limping back to Lorient with their engines in sad shape. The underground agents made sound looking welds on pressure fittings that would give way when the boat went deep. Some skippers who didn't take their boats down to maximum depth on trial runs, are on the bottom of the ocean now with their whole crews because these welds gave way under attack. Workmen drilled small holes in the tops of fuel tanks and plugged the holes with stuff that was soluble in salt water. A few days after this boat went to sea, the plug would dissolve and the boat would leave a tell-tale oil streak behind her when she submerged. It was impossible to keep secrets in a base such as Lorient. The whole life of the town revolved around the operations of the U-boat fleet and everyone in town rubbed elbows with the U-boats one way or another. The shipyard workers, of

halted, and dwelling houses ruined; the deep-sea fishing boats were moored and beached, because the fishermen either had no fuel or were afraid to put out on the mine-infested waters; all the schools were closed and the children were sent away into the country. Like them, the U-boat crews (as Arthur Harris had perceived) were moved well out of town for their R. and R. between patrols.

When the "happy time" was over, and Allied aircraft swept the skies of Europe and covered the approaches to the French Atlantic coast, the passage of the U-boats to and from their bases was always fraught with danger. They were constantly obliged to dive to escape attack, and they were guided by trawlers or patrol boats into harbour through the mine-fields, which were regularly reseeded. They came in with decks awash and flooded ballast tanks, ready for a crash dive at the first alarm; sometimes in shallow water, they stopped engines and hid among the inshore sardine boats until the RAF had gone. It was only when they reached the shelter of the pens that they were safe.

There, the scene was more reassuring, still giving

the impression of German industry and strength. A sleek row of U-boats lay in water like a millpond, contrasting strangely with the shattered buildings of the harbour town; other boats were propped up in dry dock, while local harbour gangs were working on the hulls. As the crewmen came ashore, the sound of organized activity was everywhere, and the familiar, mingled smells of seasalt, oil and paint; the walls towered around them, dripping condensation and coldly reflecting the flames of welding burners; they passed ranks of cranes and derricks, great retorts of acid for the batteries, busy teams of workers and uniformed officials who saluted their Commander. They could easily have been in Hamburg, Kiel or Wilhelmshaven.

This, however, was defeated France, apparently complacent yet potentially hostile and subversive. Most of the above-water repair work was being carried out by French technicians, and whenever some inexplicable defect in the boat revealed itself at sea, suspicions of sabotage arose—suspicions that were always impossible to prove.

course, got right down inside them. Tradesmen delivered food to the boats, and any fool could tell from their grocery orders when a boat was about to sail. A brass band met boats returning from a successful cruise and the boats came up the river proudly displaying pennants with the names of their victims printed on them for anyone to see. Bartenders, waitresses, and gals of the evening took intimate parts in the continual round of arrival and departure binges. Anyone who kept his ears open after the first five or six rounds of drinks, could pick up many items of secret official information.
—from *Twenty Million Tons Under The Sea*
by Rear Admiral Daniel V. Gallery, USN

left: Though brilliantly designed, the U-boat shelters engineered and constructed by the Todt Organization were not entirely bomb-proof as evidenced by massive holes in the roof of this pen at Brest. Three pens, in fact, had their roofs blown in by bombs of the Royal Air Force. far left: US Army personnel meet with French workers at the recently captured southwestern fire complex at the port of Brest.

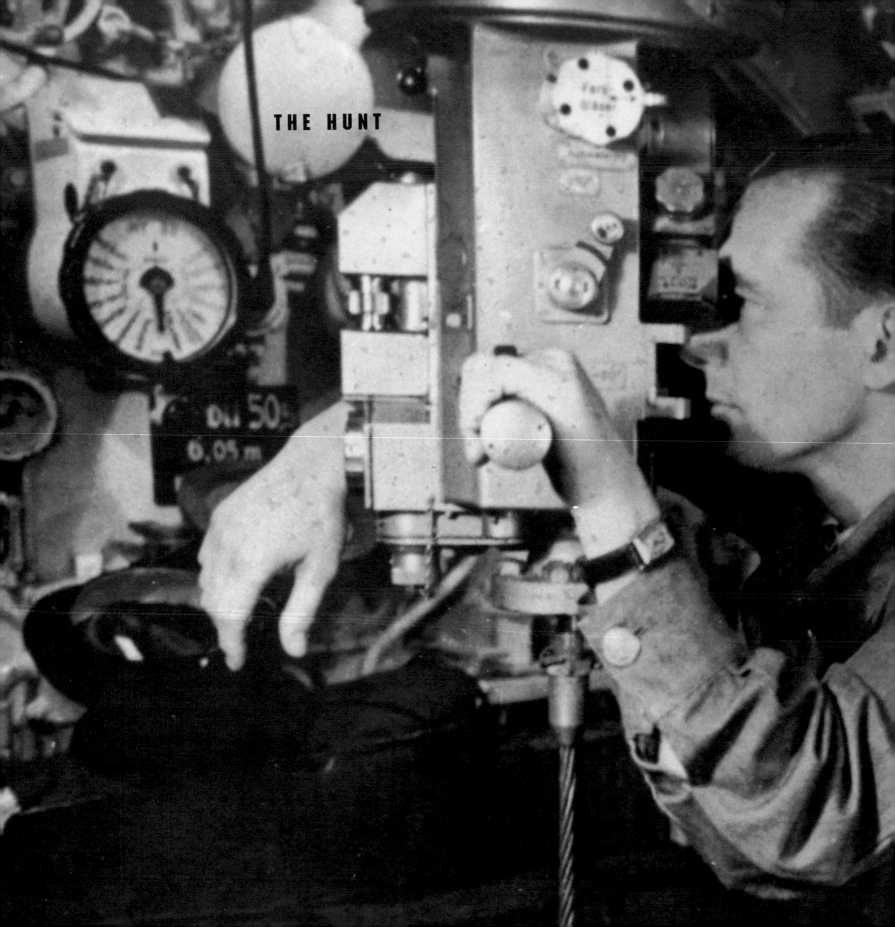

THE HUNT

AS EVERY deep-sea sailor knows, winter weather in the North Atlantic can be harsh, and January 1943 provided some of the nastiest then on record. In those few weeks, a succession of deep low-pressure zones crept across the ocean, from the east coast of America to the British Isles, bringing heavy showers of rain or of snow and raging winds that whipped the waves to enormous, heights. Between the lows, belts of higher pressure pacified the seas but engendered fog—blinding, soundless and enervating. As for its impact on the great ocean battle, the weather occupied a neutral stance: it was as hostile to the German U-boats as it was to the Allied merchant shipping and their naval escorts.

No one who crossed the Atlantic in that time was ever likely to forget it—certainly not the crew of a Type VIIC U-boat, based at Saint-Nazaire, which was one of half-a-dozen raiders searching for a convoy reported to be following the Great Circle route from Halifax to Liverpool. According to BdU, thirty more freighters, tankers and troop-ships were steaming east–north-east, somewhere in the map square defined to westward by the meridian of 32 degrees and to the south by the 55th parallel. The orders to the U-boats were that the first to sight the convoy was to signal its position to Lorient, and then to just shadow it, acting as *Fühlungshalter*—the contact boat—until the rest of the *rudel* could take up their ambush positions forward of its course.

The Commander and crew of the Saint-Nazaire U-boat neither knew nor had the need to know how BdU had learned about the convoy. The information could have come from a German agent in a neutral port, from an intercept by *B-Dienst* of Allied signals traffic or, more improbably, from aerial reconnaissance. But although they knew of the convoy's existence finding it was another matter.

Travelling on the surface, the U-boat had been pitching and tossing in heavy seas for most of the day. A thousand times the bows had gone under

The wind was rough and the sea mountainous. The motion of the boat was a perpetual swinging, swaying, rocking, rolling, and listing. Inside, the humidity was intolerable. Moisture condensing on the cold steel hull, ran in streaks into the bilges. Food turned rotten and had to be thrown overboard. Bread became soggy and mildewy. Paper dissolved. Our clothes were clammy and never dried, and whatever we touched was wet and slimy. For days we had no proper navigational fix. We could not shoot a single star, nor did we see the sun or the moon. Only the daily trim dive brought relief from rocking and spray. Down in the quiet depth we finished the work we otherwise could not perform, had a meal without losing it on the deck plates or in the bilges. And for an hour or two we recuperated while waiting for the next assault of water and wind. These routine dives were never long enough, and surfacing always came too soon.
—from *Iron Coffins*
by Herbert A. Werner

left: A surfaced boat, the *U-123*, making a hard ride in a rough sea, May 1940.

...the Commander seats himself at the periscope: a mechanical work of art, trained left and right by means of pedals. The right-hand controls an angling mirror which permits vision from 70 degrees above to 15 degrees below the horizontal. The left-hand operates a compensating lever which allows for the motion of the sea and small movements of the boat itself. A handle controls the and the propellers had reared out of the water, impotently churning empty air; the men on the bridge-watch, strapped to the rails for safety, half-blinded by the spray, caked with salt and soaking to the skin, had been relieved of their ordeal every two hours. The only consolation was that they were looking for an east-bound convoy, and every sea-mile they travelled was taking them a little nearer home. The light was just beginning to fade when the Watch Officer shouted through the voice-pipe down to the control room: "Commander to the bridge, mastheads red thirty!"

The Kapitänleutnant was with them in an instant, sou'wester pulled down, sheepskin collar up, binoculars in hand. At his command, the helmsman turned a few degrees to port. As the U-boat lifted high on a wave-top, the binoculars were focused for an instant on that distant masthead, which vanished when the bows pitched in the trough as quickly as it had appeared next time the boat was tossed up on the swell. The Commander looked again, and this time he was content. There were two vessels out there in the distance, and where there were two vessels there were always more. "Midships", he ordered, "full ahead, both."

There were a few U-boat commanders, better suited to the lone wolf role than to being members of a pack, whose chief consideration was their

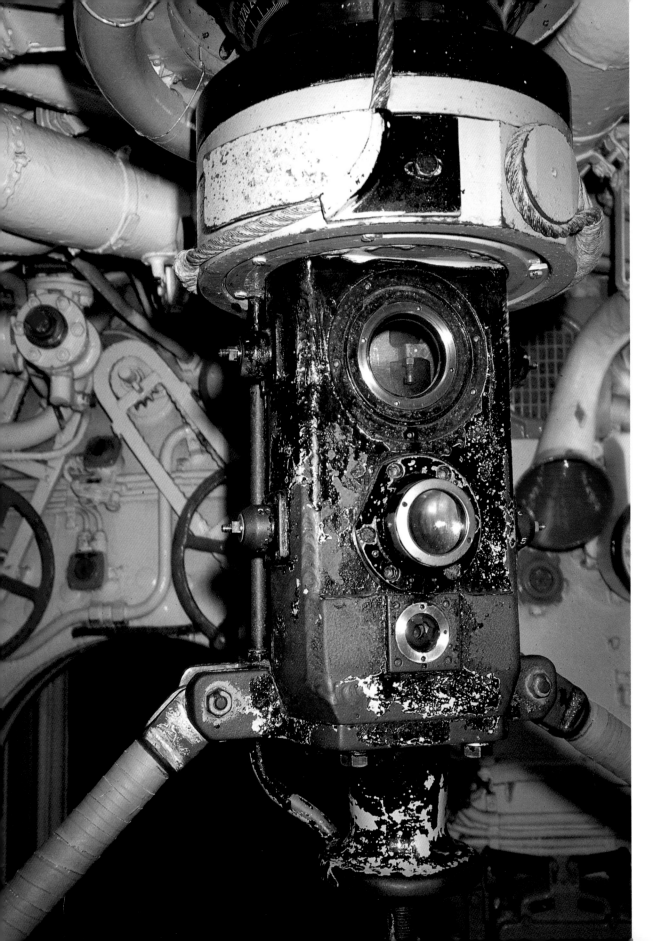

lenses, giving an alternative magnification of 1.5 or .6, with various degrees of shading against glare. In addition, a Kontax or cine-camera can be used with the periscope. The whole can be warmed, so as to prevent misting of the mirror. Obviously, the view through the periscope includes crosswires, range-scale, and bearing from a compass-repeater, while a glance upward or downward enables gunfire to be controlled with the aid of various graduated dials. The figures are coloured red, green, yellow, black or white, corresponding with the type of information they give. A torpedo firing-push is close by.

—from *U-BOAT 977* by Heinz Schaeffer

far left: Heavy-duty binoculars mounted on the torpedo aiming device of *U-373*, a Type VIIC boat out of La Pallice in April 1942. The binoculars were fastened to the torpedo aimer and the target's bearing was then automatically transmitted below. left: The control room periscope of *U-995*, a Type VIIC boat on display near the German Naval Memorial at Laboé near Kiel.

It might be true to say that the issue of the war depends on whether Hitler's U-boat attack on Allied tonnage, or the increase and application of Allied air power, reach their full fruition first. The growth of U-boat warfare and its spread to the most distant waters, as well as improvements in U-boat design, in a formidable degree must be expected. Against this may be set the increase of Allied anti-submarine craft and improvement in methods. But here is a struggle in itself.
—part of A REVIEW OF THE WAR POSITION Memorandum by the Prime Minister 21st July 1942, from *The Second World War: The Hinge of Fate* by Winston S. Churchill

personal tally of Allied shipping sunk. Having found a target, they would stealthily move in and select the fattest victim, launch their torpedoes, and as stealthily withdraw. Then, they would pass the word to BdU: "Convoy attacked in such-and-such a map square, so many vessels sunk, tonnages so-and-so, no torpedoes left, am returning to base." The Commander of the boat from Saint-Nazaire, and most of his colleagues, were no less ambitious, but were more dutiful. He knew the risks of using the

far left: The action helmsmen at their positions. left: Manning the Group Listening Device, this crewman times the run of a torpedo with a stop watch. German torpedo reliability was uneven, causing many a miss. below: No miss here.

radio: his signals could be picked up by the enemy's "Huff-duff", his position fixed and flashed to all the escort warships, not to mention several hundred hostile aircraft. Nevertheless, it was his duty to report the sighting and to home the others in. He sent the coded signal and was duly ordered to assume the contact role. Alternatively plunging and rising with the seas, the U-boat tracked the convoy, and the crew prepared for action.

The news of the sighting would resound in Lorient and probably Berlin; in their warm, clean offices, well-dressed, well-fed Admirals, Commodores and Captains would pore over maps, meet in earnest conference and compose exhortatory messages. But the outcome of the

The sea speaks a language polite people never repeat. It is a colossal scavenger slang and has no respect.
—from *Two Nocturnes*
by Carl Sandburg

far left: *The Sinking of the SS Bedoin*, by John Hamilton. left: One of the two surviving bomb-proof 'Dom' bunkers at the Lorient U-boat base.

mission did not rest on them; it rested on the stamina and skill of some dirty, scruffy seamen sealed in stinking steel tubes a thousand miles from home. It was like the mounting of a heavy bomber mission far out over Germany: once all the business of planning, provisioning and briefing was complete, the success or failure of the venture depended entirely on the efforts of a few hundred isolated men.

A number of those shore-based officers, serving on the headquarters staffs of the flotillas and the fleet, had themselves taken part in just the sort of operation that was being mounted in the North Atlantic. As they waited for the wolfpack to assemble, they recalled their feelings in the days when they were out there, in boats just such as those, creeping towards their target across the darkening sea, and they recalled the forebodings and the thrill.

Watchman, what of the night?
—Isaiah, XXI. II

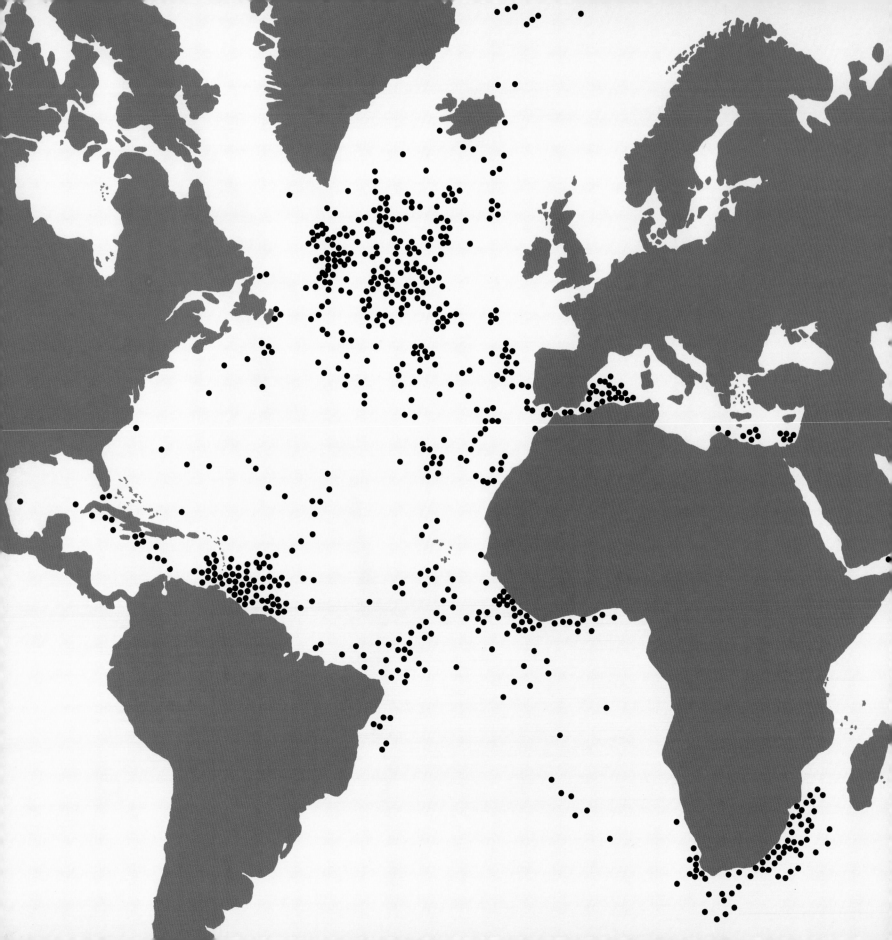

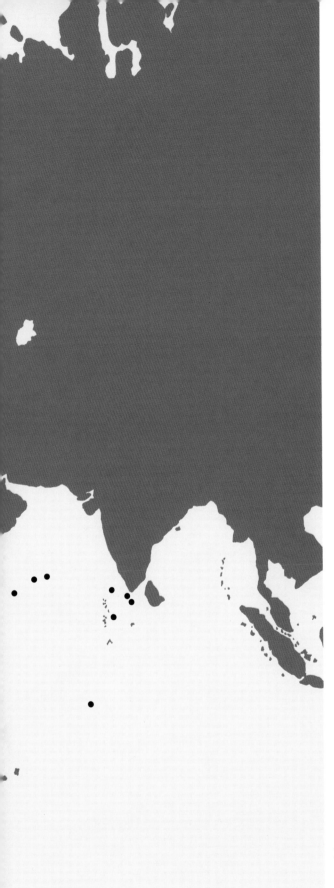

Some of them were wishing that they were there again, to be in on the climax of the hunt, to take part in the action, to see everything that happened when the attack began, but others were glad they were not. For no one who had not witnessed it himself could have the least conception of the scene, of its lurid drama, its kaleidoscopic horror. No layman could imagine the magnitude of carnage—the vast spouts of water thrown high like giant fountains, ammunition ships erupting like volcanoes, great sheets of metal hurled into the air, the hellish infernos that were stricken tankers, the towering clouds of black smoke tinged with red, the bright flare of star-shells, the streams of tracer bullets, the flickering of the Aldis lamps, the beams of questing searchlights, all accompanied by the boom of detonations, the pounding of the engines, the swishing of the screws, the awful cries of seamen drowning in the burning sea.

No such dreadful images were foremost in the minds of the Saint-Nazaire crew—few of them would see the action, anyway. Since the first sighting, some eight hours earlier, they had shadowed the convoy at a prudent distance, only submerging occasionally for the sound man to keep check of the bearing, always ready for a crash dive if one of the prowling escorts should approach. Now, the pack had gathered, the moderate, gently rolling sea was suited to their purpose—not so rough that it would be hard for the Chief to trim the boat, nor so smooth that their wake could be observed. They were within striking distance, two of the bow tubes had been opened to the ocean, two "eels" were programmed and ready for firing. They were only waiting for the order, and at last it came.

Standing in the conning tower, staring through the master sight, the Commander spoke the words: "Rohr eins—Lloss! Rohr zwei—Lloss!" Down went the firing levers, and the "eels" were on their way. "Torpedoes running", said the sound man, listening on the hydrophone. The hunt was over: the killing had begun.

Wake, friend, from forth thy lethargy! The drum / Beats brave and loud in Europe, and bids come / All that dare rouse: or are not loth to quit /
Their vicious ease, and be o'erwhelmed with it. / It is a call to keep the spirits alive / That gasp for action, and would yet revive / Man's buried honour, in his sleepy life.
—from *An Epistle To A Friend, To Persuade Him To The Wars*
by Ben Jonson

The people who get on in this world are the people who get up and look for the circumstances they want, and, if they can't find them, make them.
—from *Mrs. Warren's Profession*
by George Bernard Shaw

The chart at left shows the approximate locations of merchant ships sunk by U-boats from August 1942 to May 1943 and represents a wartime assessment that does not precisely conform to the verified post-war totals.

ALARRRM!

When water covers the
head, a hundred fathoms
are as one.
—Persian proverb

Cheer up, the worst is yet
to come.
—Philander Johnson

right: Seawater pours
into the control room of
U-101 as an Alarm dive
is initiated in April 1941.

IN THE North Atlantic, on a fine spring morning in 1943, the U-boat is heading west–north-west, running on the surface at a steady fourteen knots. She is about 1,200 sea miles from her base at Saint-Nazaire, and her Commander's orders are to join forces with five more boats of his flotilla, and to intercept an east-bound Allied convoy that sailed out of Halifax seven days ago. The Commander and the 1st and 2nd Watch Officers, the bosun, four petty officers and half-a-dozen seamen are experienced campaigners; for the rest of the complement, this is their first operational patrol. The boat is carrying a full load of torpedoes and deck ammunition, adequate provisions and sufficient fuel for ten days on station before she must return.

At 0740 hours, the forward deck-watch points a finger and shouts "Destroyer, green twenty, Sir!" Flicking his cigarette into the ocean, the 1st Officer quickly raises his binoculars and trains them on the horizon above the starboard bow. There, in three-quarter profile, is the sleek shape of the sub-hunter, her smoke-stacks trailing a long, black plume as she swings toward them. He mutters a curse—a damnation of radar and of prying Tommi aircraft—leans into the tower and shouts into the speaking tube: "Alarm dive!" and at once, the klaxon sounds throughout the boat. Close upon each other, the watch slide down the ladder into the control room, ignoring the rungs and braking their descent with knees and elbows on the stanchions; the top lid shuts behind them, and No.1 spins the hand-wheel to make it watertight.

Quickly as they move, a lot of the Atlantic finds its way into their boat—through the hatch and the speaking tube and periscope gaskets. "Twenty metres", says the Commander, and the Chief Engineer raps out the commands. The diesel engines stop, the intakes and the exhausts close, the electric motors hum as the gears engage and battery power takes over.

In the control room, the main vent levers are pulled down, the ballast tanks are open and the air rushes out, roaring like a gale. "All hands forward", is the order, and the stokers from the engine room move at the double, crouching as they pass through the bulkhead doors and hatches. The Chief's orders to the seamen at the hydroplane controls are carefully measured and deliberate: dive too steeply and the stern will rear out of the water and, like an aircraft in a stall, the boat will fail to answer the controls. Now the hydroplanes tilt, the bows tip smoothly down and the U-boat slips below the surface; with only a momentary trail of bubbles to show that it was ever there.

The destroyer's approach comes as no surprise to the Commander or to the seasoned members of the crew: they have been expecting it, ever since the big twin-engined aeroplane flew in from the north-east and began an orbit at 1,000 feet. They had dived immediately, but they knew the chances were that the aircraft's crew had seen them and would pass their position to the nearest Allied warship. The sighting of the aircraft, however, had been more than an hour ago, and no attack had followed, so they had blown the water ballast and come up, first to fourteen metres for the search periscope, and then, when the Commander had scanned the entire horizon, to the surface to resume the hunt. Now, as so often, the positions are reversed: the hunter has become the prey.

Twenty metres down, the boat is trimmed, the crew are at action stations. The electric motors are barely turning over, providing just sufficient power to give the helmsman headway. The sound man sits at the hydrophone controls, adjusting the receiver, trying to penetrate the sea sounds to find the patter of the destroyer's asdic, then to tune in exactly to read off the bearing. The Commander stands close by, with one foot in the control room and the other in the passage beside the sound man's shack. The boat is rigged for quiet running; men move stealthily, what few words are needed are spoken in low tones, the auxiliary machinery is stilled, and all of the non-essential electrics are

A depth charge must explode almost in contact with the tough pressure hull of a sub to get a kill. It takes some seconds for a depth charge to arch through the air and more seconds to sink through the water to its set depth, during which time a skillful sub skipper may maneuver out from under it. If he chooses to go down to say five hundred feet, he has quite a few seconds for his evasive maneuvering. If you miss him once he has that fifteen minutes reprieve during which he doesn't have to creep silently but can run at high speed while the ocean is reverberating and disturbed water conditions give your sonar phony echoes.

...after a salvo of ashcans explodes all around him, maybe it takes the skipper's nerves that long to settle down too. While they are still agitated he *may* do something foolish. So the standard procedure at this time was to fire a salvo of hedgehogs as you approached the sub and if you got no explosion as you continued your run, to plant a garden of ashcans around him. In perhaps half the sub killings during the Battle of the Atlantic, the whole action was fought without either side actually seeing the enemy. The battle begins with a radar blip or a sonar contact on the Allied side, and a hydrophone or Naxos warning on the German side. An hour or so later it

ends with a blazing surface ship upending and sinking, or a great puddle of oil spreading out across the ocean with pieces of submarine junk in the middle of it.
—from *Twenty Million Tons Under The Sea*
by Rear Admiral Daniel V. Gallery, USN

Valor is a gift. Those having it never know for sure whether they have it till the test comes. And those having it in one test never know for sure if they will have it when the next test comes.
—Carl Sandburg

Courage is resistance to fear, mastery of fear—not absence of fear.
—Mark Twain

Character is what you are in the dark.
—from *Sermons*
by Dwight L. Moody

far right: The U-bunker at Saint-Nazaire.

feed the guns with WAR BONDS and help to end the War

switched off.

"Propeller noises zero-five-zero degrees," says the sound man, and the Captain nods. "Steer three-twenty," he tells the helmsman, "go to fifty metres, slow ahead both."

They hear the quick, even rhythm of the enemy destroyer's screws, and the U-boat sways as she goes by. They wait for the depth charges that are sure to follow, and do not have long to wait. The explosions sound like gun-shots, the sea roars in to fill the gaping voids they make, and the U-boat rocks and shakes. "Eighty metres", orders the Commander, and down they go again. For three minutes, the boat runs at an angle to the destroyer's bearing and doubles back again. The Commander is weaving, in a slow-motion, underwater version of

a bomber pilot's corkscrew when he is trying to dodge the searchlights and radar-guided flak.

Still the *Wasserbomben* follow them, terrifyingly near. The blast waves are thunderous, putting out the lights, cracking glass on instruments, smashing a chronometer; crockery, utensils, and every article not well-secured is hurled onto the planks, and everything that will break does just that. A pipe splits amidships, and a jet of water spurts across the control room until the leak is plugged. The beams of torchlights palely light the scene until the auxiliary lighting switches on. The Chief prowls the boat with a petty officer, seeking any signs of fracture in the plates.

To the beleaguered crewmen, each detonation is like a personal assault: a kick in the kidneys, a punch in the stomach, a hard slap in the face. Saliva tastes of iron, sweat smells of fear; men holding onto stanchions, wedge themselves in angles and try to make their bodies small and inconspicuous...but there is nowhere for anyone to hide. Every man knows that, any minute, one of those detonations can crack the hull and that all of them will die; those who have been through this ordeal before open their mouths wide to equalize the pressure in their sinuses and save their eardrums.

The boat is lying at 125 metres, and that is deeper than she is supposed to go. The water pressure at this depth is 235 pounds per square inch, and there are so many weak points for the sea to penetrate: inlets and exhausts, hatches, glands and vents. Even the steel skin of the pressure hull must be bending inwards in between the spars. They cannot use the ventilators, so the air is motionless; the destroyer's sonar would pick up the sound of pumping, and her look-outs would see the oily bubbles on the surface, so the bilge stays in the boat. The temperature rises and the atmosphere is foul; the crewmen are as motionless as possible to conserve oxygen.

For all his studied nonchalance, the U-boat

Commander is concerned. He knows this siege of his fragile underwater citadel can go on for hours, and even days. In time, the oxygen will fail, the batteries will run dry and, without them, the boat will sink until it rests on the sea-bed, some two thousand metres down.

"Screws bearing zero-four-five, sir", says the sound man, "and getting louder".

The Commander nods to the Chief, and the electric motors hum. "Steer zero-five-zero," orders the U-boat Commander, "slow ahead both." He is presenting the boat's narrowest silhouette to the approaching asdic. The sonar pulses ping louder and faster against the hull, and the whole crew can hear them. A wire short-circuits with a shower of sparks; a flicker of flame and a sudden acrid smell are enough to awaken the men's most basic fear, until an electrician throws a switch and a rating quells the flame.

The Commander takes the boat deeper, down to 150 metres, and calls for full power from the motors. "Steer twenty port", he tells the helmsman. He is trying to outguess the man on the bridge of the enemy destroyer. They are playing a listening game—listen, move a little, stop and listen, move again. If the destroyer's captain could have heaved to above the U-boat's last position and dropped his depth-charges from directly overhead, the battle would have ended then and there, but his asdic searches at an angle, not immediately below.

The attack goes on relentlessly, and the sound

All these tidal gatherings, growth and decay / Shining and darkening are forever Renewed; and the whole cycle impenitently / Revolves, and all the past is future: Make it a difficult world...for practical people.
—from *Practical People* by Robinson Jeffers

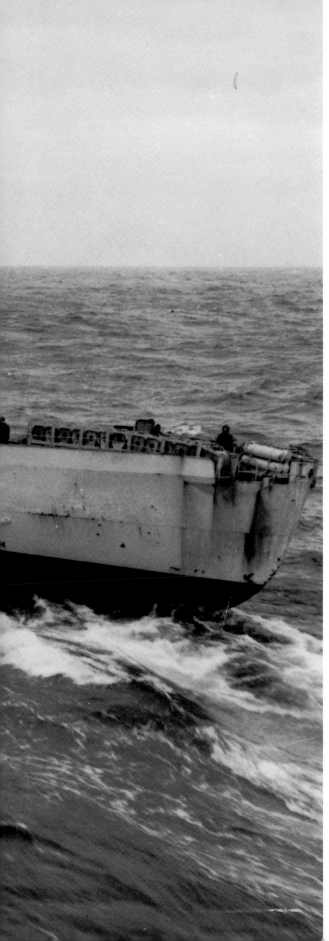

man keeps a running tally of the detonations. The U-boat is driven ever deeper, and water from leakages rises to a dangerous level in the electric motor room. Buckets are passed from hand to hand, carrying the water to the forward bilges, and the bows go down. The heads cannot be vented, so the doors are locked; for men who must urinate, cans are passed around, and invariably spill, adding their odour to the noxious air and their contents to the rising tide that swills across the planks. To be in the fore-ends is like living in a sewer. Water in the batteries produces chlorine gas, and to protect their lungs and mucous membranes the men clamp their nostrils and suck filtered air through rubber hoses.

Such traumatic times can cause hysteria or acute neurosis, known in the U-boat arm as the *Blechkoller*—literally "tin can frenzy". There are men who have wept and others who have screamed, and it is not unknown for a seaman (or indeed an airman), in a time of deadly fear, involuntarily to soil himself—an event of small significance in the context of all that is then happening but personally shaming and no aid to a morale already under stress.

It is hard to tell which is the greater danger—the enemy's depth charges or the elemental pressure. The shipbuilder's version of the maximum diving depth is more like an opening bid in an auction sale than a scientific calculation—everybody knows it has often been exceeded. The only question is, how deep is too deep? There was a report of one boat that actually resurfaced from 280 metres, but the only men who really know how far down a boat can go before the water crushes it will always keep the secret to themselves.

It is many hours later that the sound man pulls a headphone off one ear, looks at the Commander and manages a smile. "Propeller noises receding, sir," he reports, "bearing three-four-zero."

The Commander nods and wipes the sweat from his eyes. "Good", he says, "we'll wait a little while, to make quite sure they're not playing games with us."

The English country gentleman galloping after a fox—the unspeakable in full pursuit of the uneatable.
—from *A Woman of No Importance*
by Oscar Wilde

"Alarrrmmm!" The Captain's call was drowned in the shriek of the bell. *U-557* dipped her bow into the inky sea. Simultaneously a thunderous explosion lifted the boat by the stern, shook her violently, and turned her wildly off her axis. *U-557* was out of control. She fell fast. Three charges exploded, seemingly just above the conning tower. After each shattering roar, the hull moaned, the floor plates jumped and kicked our feet, wood splintered, glass disintegrated, food cans flew through the boat; then all was black for long seconds until the emergency lighting came on again. But the hull itself held tight. Only the gaskets and seats of many valves had loosened, letting water trickle into the bilges in countless little streams. The force of the detonations had pressed the boat deeper, and the influx of water drove her still closer to the limit of her design.
—from *Iron Coffins*
by Herbert A. Werner

The crew are still silent, but the relaxation of tension in the boat can almost be felt. Men whose eyes have either been shut tight, or focused on eternity, now glance at one another with a grimace of relief. The moments now pass slowly until the Commander glances at his watch. "Take her up, Chief," he says, "periscope depth." The men move to their stations, the E-motors hum and the ballast tanks are blown. Slowly the boat climbs out of the depths, the water column in the Papenberg sinks, and the hull plates creak as the pressure drops. At forty feet, the masthead breaks the surface, and the Chief balances the boat, "hanging on the periscope".

The Commander climbs into the conning tower, sits astride the saddle with the periscope shaft between his knees, his feet on the pedals and his cheeks pressed against the rubber moulding of the sight. Keeping the scope head just above the surface, he turns slowly through 360 degrees. Now and then he stops, turns back a little, stays rigid for a moment, while the men who are watching hold their breath, then he continues the rotation. At last he sits back, snaps the handles shut, looks at the Chief and points a finger up.

The tower breaks the surface, the decks stream water, and the watch climb to the bridge. Up there in the daylight, it is a moment for each of them to savour—to know that life remains after what had seemed like certain death. There is still a sky above and a rolling sea around them; the boat is still afloat, and they are all alive. The impact of fresh air is like an anaesthetic, and it is only with an effort that they keep their wits. The Commander is suddenly beside them on the bridge. "How long must I wait", he raps, "for full reports of damage?"

"At once, Herr Kaleu." The inspections reveal that an aerial has gone, bridge rails are bent, the conning tower is pitted and one of the Oerlikons may never fire again. The Chief reports a problem with the after hydroplanes. As for the hull, rivets have popped and bolts have been sheared, but the pressure skin is sound. Considering the battering

they took, it could be a great deal worse. It is only the machine-gun that cannot be repaired. For now, the bilges can be emptied, the foul air can escape, the accumulation of human waste and debris can be jettisoned, and sodden clothes can dry on hot pipes in the engine room. More importantly, the batteries can be charged. The pistons pound, familiar blue vapour curls up from the exhausts, as the diesel engines begin to drive the boat.

At the all-purpose bunk-cum-table in the wardroom, the Commander is studying the map. It shows the navigator's best attempts to chart the boat's eccentric courses during the alarm. The Commander draws a line to the north-east. Somewhere out there, the convoy is slowly steaming on. Their duty is to find it and, as exhorted by their Admiral, "Attack, attack, attack!" They still have their torpedoes and more than half their fuel.

The cypher machine is placed on the table, and a signal for BdU is drafted, dated and encoded. "Counter-attack by destroyer, slight damage, resuming patrol."

Necessity makes even the
timid brave.
—Sallust

When your neighbour's
house is afire your own
property is at stake.
—Horace

TITTLE TATTLE
LOST THE BATTLE

far left: Testing escape
apparatus. left: The
evident strain of the
ongoing danger and the
awful oppressiveness of
a combat submarine's
confining structure.

MADDENING
ROUTINE

THE LIFE of a U-boat man at sea consisted of two parts—on watch and off watch. The duration of these phases depended on his trade: a technician stood two watches of six hours each, and a seaman three of four hours—from midnight to four o'clock, four to eight o'clock, and so on through the day. Only the cook was excused the watch, and that was with good reason: he had to produce three meals a day for each of the watches, and that important duty, constantly interrupted by the movement of his crew mates through the narrow galley, was enough to keep him busy for every waking hour.

The First and Second Lieutenants, and the navigator or quartermaster (usually a Chief Petty Officer), each stood a watch in turn, accompanied by a Petty Officer and two seamen. The four-hour deck-watch would probably be halved in the very worst of weather, when big seas swept the decks in solid sheets of water, and the rain came at the bridge horizontally, vertically and diagonally. In these conditions no amount of clothing—neither oilskin coats and leather trousers, sou'westers over Balaclava helmets, double pairs of socks inside the sea-boots, nor sweaters with towels wrapped round the neck—could prevent a man being frozen to the marrow and soaked to the skin within minutes of taking up his post. It was in that sort of weather, aided by a sudden gale and a following sea, that the entire deck-watch of *U-106* was swept away by a monster wave. No one was aware of it until a control room hand had cause to go aloft.

A U-boat crewman, like a flier in a heavy bomber, lived a life that combined similar but unequal periods of boredom and tedium, terror and excitement. The difference lay in the time scale: the flier measured his in hours and minutes, the seaman in weeks and hours. In a way, the on-and-off watch routine could be reassuring: each man knew his duty and where he had to be at any time of day or night. It could also be maddening in its sameness and predictability: hour after hour of

Good company in a journey makes the way seem the shorter.
—from *The Compleat Angler* by Izaak Walton

The only way to have a friend is to be one.
—from *Of Friendship* by Ralph Waldo Emerson

right: Foul-weather gear was essential aboard a U-boat on patrol. The standard oilskins were frequently worn by all in most conditions, but heavy-weather gear (far right) was often required as well.

136

Some of us, regarding the ocean with understanding and affection, have seen it looking old, as if the immemorial ages had been stirred up from the undisturbed bottom of ooze. For it is a gale of wind that makes the sea look old.
—from *The Mirror of the Sea*
by Joseph Conrad

below: A German military medical kit.

staring at horizons, listening through headphones, recharging batteries, watching dials and gauges, greasing, cleaning and, when not so occupied, peeling potatoes. Even the diversions—the fire drills, the escape drills, attack drills, trim-test dives, practice with the guns, simulated crash dives with the officers taking turns—even these became matters of tedious routine.

When the boat was on the surface in a choppy sea, with the induction valves closed to keep the water out and the diesel engines breathing inboard air, the inboard atmosphere was stifling and the temperature could rise to 120 degrees Fahrenheit. Fresh water was only available for drinking and cooking; no one shaved unless the Commander was a crank, and nobody bathed, except in a bucket, perhaps for months on end. Clothes stank of sweat and diesel oil, and no amount of washing could ever make them clean. Grey shirts were favoured because they did not advertise the dirt. To mitigate the smells, men dabbed lemon cologne on salt-caked faces, rubbed fragrant waters in greasy, matted hair and used oily unguents to cleanse dirty skin. Despite the help of pills and castor oil, constipation was endemic; teeth and gums suffered from the lack of skilled attention, and gingivitis was a chronic ailment. Not many crewmen retained all their teeth for long.

Whenever the boat rose to the surface after being submerged, perhaps for many hours, a dirty yellow cloud would flow out of the conning tower, and a queue of seamen would form in the control room below the open hatch, holding up their pallid faces to inhale the clean sea air, and waiting for permission to take a turn on deck; there, they could relieve their aching bladders into the wide Atlantic and perhaps enjoy a cigarette—an indulgence that, unlike their British counterparts, they were normally denied within the boat.

The eyes of the U-boat were on the bridge, where the men on watch, like the gunners in a bomber's turrets, maintained an ever-roving eye: sideways and back across their sector of the ocean as far as the horizon, up, down and around the piece of sky above. As with the gunners in bombers flying by day, the watch into sunlight was not only the most taxing on the eyes, but they faced the direction from which a combat-wise attacker was most likely to approach.

The word from the Admiral was "he who sees first has won", and all around the compass, any sort of sighting had to be checked. Was that a lump of nimbo-stratus dead ahead or a smudge of smoke from an approaching warship's stacks? Was that a seagull on the starboard quarter at two-hundred feet or a Catalina flying-boat at four thousand? Up with the binoculars again—binoculars that seemed to weigh more by the hour. Those people in the Zeiss factory clearly never had to take a sea-watch.

For the men on watch, there was little time to marvel at the spectacle of twilight or dawn, or at the

ever-changing spectrum of colours, light and shade that came between. It was not for them to enjoy the summer evenings when the decks seemed to be gilded, nor to wonder at the savage splendour of a great electric storm, when jagged streaks of lightning flashed between the ocean and the lurid sky; they could not allow themselves to gaze at Aurora Borealis, spectrally glinting in the northern sky, nor at the distant beauty of the constellations overhead. Any such deviance from strict concentration was sure to be noticed by the officer of the watch, and to earn a sharp reproof.

If the U-boat's eyes were on the bridge and its heart in the control room, its ears were in the radio and hydrophone shacks and its sinews in the engine room. When the boat submerged it was entirely blind, and then only the sound waves, coming through the headphones from an array of microphones fixed underneath the bows, could give warning of vessels within range. The "sound man"

could read the vessel's bearing and judge whether it was closing or moving away; in optimum conditions, on the quarters or the beam, he could detect a single ship at a distance of about twelve miles, and the sound of a convoy could be heard at sixty. When the U-boat was submerged, he was one man who always had the ear of the Commander. On the surface, the hydrophone was ineffective, and when the boat was snorkelling, the roar of the engines blotted out all sound. Aft in the engine room, with the diesels running, the noise was absolutely deafening, and the mechanics used their own sign language for communication.

The radio telegraphist came into action when the boat was on the surface and short-wave messages could be transmitted and received. Then, it was his task to send reports of attacks and counter-attacks to BdU—U-boat headquarters—with the boat's position, its torpedo and fuel states, the sea conditions and the weather, and to receive deployment orders in return; between times, he would listen in on signals sent from other U-boats in the wolfpack and, whenever possible, eavesdrop on messages from the merchant ships.

Thoughtful commanders (and Kapitänleutnant Otto Kretschmer was one such) routinely submerged for two hours or so before dawn, with two purposes in mind. First, to facilitate the use of the hydrophone and so avoid collision with vessels that might approach unnoticed in the dark; and second, being mindful of the stresses on the crew, to allow them to relax, get cleaned up and eat their breakfast undisturbed. Mealtimes on the surface, especially in rough weather, tended to be messy affairs; food in transit from the galley sometimes failed to reach its destination in one piece, and the guard rails or "fiddles" fitted to tables, might save the crockery but not always the contents.

Kretschmer's fellow-commander, Günther Prien, could be less considerate. He had a degree of arrogance that was sometimes evident in young men of his breeding and was no great

disadvantage in the role that he sustained throughout his brilliant career, although it might not have made him welcome in a Royal Navy wardroom. As an example of his style, he would order harbour exercises for his crew in between patrols, in which he did not join. His crew respected him, but there was no need for them to love him. The public did love him, but they did not really know him and Dönitz, who favoured him, never had to sail with him.

Under water, the U-boat moved smoothly and almost in silence; on the surface it pitched and tossed with the motion of the sea, rearing onto great wave crests and swooping into troughs, twisting and rolling in the cross seas; the rhythmic pounding of the diesels, the singing of the jump wire on the fore-deck and the constant slap of waves against the hull were sounds as eternally monotonous as, to an airman, were the growl of aero-engines, the whistle of the aerials, and the howl of slipstream tearing at the fuselage.

However stalwart he might be through attacks from the air or from the sea, however hardy in the freezing hours on watch, the U-boat sailor's morale could be sapped by the infuriating, constantly repeated habits of his mess-mates. There was the radio man who played the same dreary waltz tune by the hour on the phonograph, there was the stoker who, at every meal, picked his teeth with a table fork and swallowed what he picked; and there was the mixer, who gave a stiff Nazi salute after each resounding fart. And as if human behaviour were not annoying enough, three or four French flies, a thousand miles from base, were always there at meal-times and when a man was trying to sleep, somehow evading every swipe, and providing an irritating lesson in the art of survival to everyone on board.

Conversation in the crew's quarters sometimes tended to be ribald, or even downright obscene, as it always has been and perhaps always will be among groups of servicemen when they are together.

Shipboard routine had replaced the excitement of the chase and the battle. And it was a maddening routine. The small ship rolled and slapped, listed and shuddered endlessly. Utensils, spare parts, tools, and conserves showered down on us continually; porcelain cups and dishes shattered on the deck-plates and in the bilges as we ate our meals directly out of cans. The men, penned up together in the rocking, sweating drum, took the motion and the monotony with stoicism. Occasionally, someone's temper flared, but spirits remained high. We were all patient veterans. Everyone aboard looked alike, smelled alike, had adopted the same phrases and curses. We had learned to live together in a narrow tube no longer than two railroad cars. We tolerated each other's faults and became experts on each other's habits— how everyone laughed and snarled, talked and snored, sipped his coffee and caressed his beard. The pressure mounted with the passage of each uneventful day, but it could be relieved in an instant by the sight of a fat convoy.
—from *Iron Coffins* by Herbert A. Werner

left: Attachment to the jumping wire provided some safety on deck.

right: Exercise offered a rare respite from the normal routine. This is *U-107*, a Type IXB boat commanded in July 1942 by Kapitänleutnant Gelhaus. far right: The diesel motor room of the *U-65*, September 1940. below: A still from the film *Das Boot*.

U-22 tilted violently as the diving planes angled down and the rush of water into the ballast tanks roared like thunder inside the boat. Hashagen had given orders to level out at 50 feet but, due to an unexpected fault in the depth rudder, the U-boat plunged below the 50 feet mark and kept falling. 'She tilted up and down like a rocking-horse, sinking now by the head and then by the stern—but always sinking.' Hoppe rushed into the control room but with the British cruiser lying in wait on the surface he did not dare to blow the ballast tanks and *U-22* was at the mercy of her broken rudder. When the submarine reached 200 feet the situation was fast becoming serious for, at that depth, the pressure of the sea would crush the steel hull like a matchbox. Already the metal was groaning under the strain, the steel support beams were beginning to buckle and tiny beads of water glistened around unseated rivets. But something even more terrifying was happening in the cramped confines of the battery compartment. 'Everything else lost its importance...I caught the acrid smell of chlorine gas and everyone was coughing, spluttering, and choking,' Hashagen recalled. Sea water, forcing its way through the seams, had mixed with the sulphuric acid of the

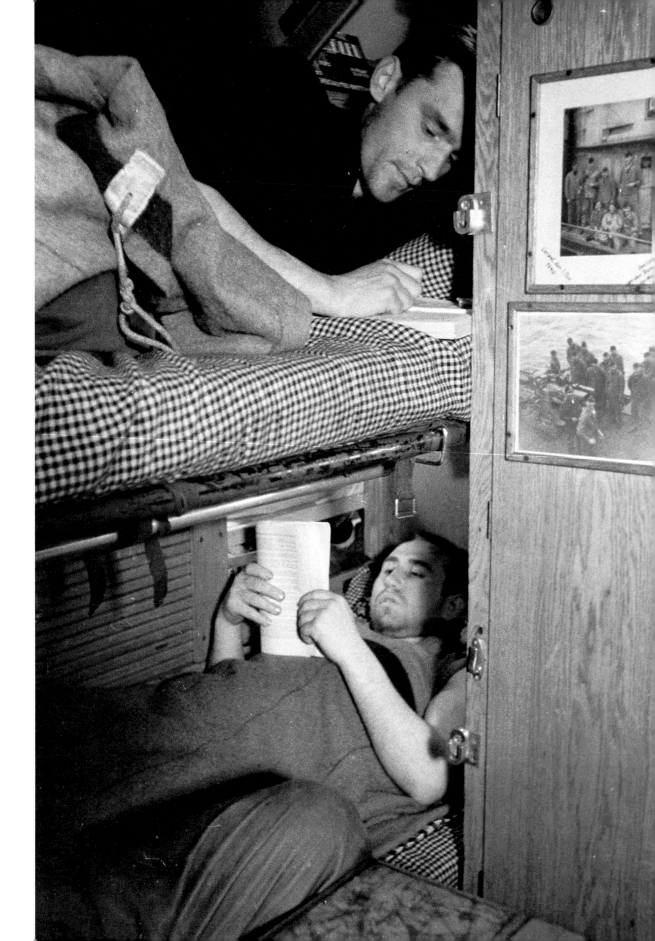

Sexual experiences, whether real or imagined, were described in detail and at length, liaisons planned for the next return to port were lasciviously envisaged, Winston Churchill was routinely reviled, desk-bound officers of the Flotilla staff were savagely derided, and even the Führer did not escape calumny (although woe betide the officer who was openly critical of the Hitler regime—one bold U-boat commander, reported to have been thus, was promptly arraigned and shot). As in any close-knit group, jesting insults were exchanged, usually accepted in the spirit they were meant and as pointedly returned, but occasionally a remark might open up a wound and cause disproportionate and rankling offence.

From the early days of 1943 the crew could listen, on various frequencies and several times a week, to broadcasts by "Commander Robert Lee Norden" (the *nom de guerre* of a German-speaking US Navy officer). He would tell of appalling losses in the U-boat arm, giving names and numbers, and describe how ill-advisedly their campaign was led, as well as mentioning disgusting scandals among the Nazi Party hierarchy, insisting how well all would be but for Adolf Hitler's insane lust for conquest. This was all seemingly backed up by solid evidence, and spoken soberly as though by a friend. The British had been waging a similar war of words from "Radio Atlantic", which, while purporting to emanate from a resistance movement in the heart of Germany, was actually being broadcast from the Duke of Bedford's stately home at Woburn Abbey. Both propaganda efforts attracted a wide audience, in the same way as William Joyce, or "Lord Haw-Haw", talking from Berlin, drew many Britons to their wireless sets, sometimes for the sheer fun of it, and sometimes to say "Blimey, he's right, you know!"

To maintain a high morale among men who are liable to be killed at any time, but who must be persuaded to carry on the fight, has always been a problem and a test of leadership. Any attempt to conceal or minimize the danger will soon be seen as false, and mistrust of the leader will surely follow; history has shown that sometimes the best course is to state the danger plainly, and say "whatever is to come, we'll face it together, and in the end we'll win". That was how Winston Churchill heartened and inspired the British people, in their darkest hour, with his open acknowledgement that "blood, toil, tears and sweat" would precede their victory.

For the Anglo-Saxon races, if not for the Teutonic, a leavening of humour, possibly macabre, has often been helpful in living through adversity, as music-hall comedians and press cartoonists have long been aware. The fighting man employs and enjoys this kind of humour, but he needs something more to maintain his spirit and stiffen his resolve; at times he is sustained by the knowledge that his target is attainable, that what is asked of him is possible, and that his life will not be wasted in a hopeless cause. At other times, and perhaps for other men, an effective stimulus could be provided by what Shakespeare wrote of in *Henry V* as "a touch of Harry in the night"—a word from the leader to show that he considered the welfare of his men, to show that he knew them, or at least some of them, by name, and that he knew about their families and cared about them too.

The good U-boat commander was well aware of the requirement for occasional respites from the maddening routine, as any able leader should be. He would try to ensure that the boat's library was adequately stocked, that someone aboard could play the accordion or the harmonica, that—*pace* the Nazi propagandists—the stock of phonograph records were of a sort the seamen liked; if someone had a birthday he would throw an *ad hoc* party in the fore-ends, with the cook's best effort at a cake, a bottle of beer and perhaps a little cognac. Such simple, small diversions could be like shafts of sunlight piercing heavy cloud; they could encourage the belief that normal life went on, even in that strange, lonely world below the sea.

batteries and was sending off clouds of greenish-yellow vapour. 'I don't think there is anything that will strike such fear in a submarine man as the thought of being trapped in the iron hull while choking gas seeps from the batteries bit by bit. No death could be more agonizing.'
—from *The Killing Time The U-boat War 1914–18* by Edwyn A. Gray

A man may have strong humanitarian and democratic principles; but if he happens to have been brought up as a bath-taking, shirt-changing lover of fresh air, he will have to overcome certain physical repugnances before he can bring himself to put those principles into practice.
—from *Jesting Pilate* by Aldous Huxley

A gossip is one who talks to you about others; a bore is one who talks to you about himself; and a brilliant conversationalist is one who talks to you about yourself.
—Lisa Kirk, New York *Journal-American*

THE RUSSIAN RUN

If there's a dish / For which I wish / More frequent than the rest / If there's a food On which I brood / When starving or depressed, / If there's a thing that life can give / Which makes it worth our while to live, / If there's an end / On which I'd spend / My last remaining cash, / It's sausage, friend, / It's sausage, friend, / It's sausage, friend, and mash.
—from *Sausage and Mash* by A.P. Herbert

right: *Convoy to Russia*, by Charles Pears.

ONE OF THE FEW occasions when Germany's U-boats, surface ships and aircraft successfully combined in an attack on Allied shipping was in July 1942, when a convoy bound for Russia was engaged at the half-way point of its 2,500-mile voyage. As it happened, the big ships were not required to act—their mere presence was enough to seal the convoy's fate. It was one of the grimmest episodes of the war at sea.

Of the two routes to Russia—north, by the fringes of the Arctic Circle, and south, through the Persian Gulf—the northern route was the shorter from any British port. Since they started sailing in the autumn of 1941, the convoys from Britain had carried cargoes of guns, ammunition, oil, explosives, trucks, aircraft and spare parts to aid the Russian forces; mounting and escorting them had provided a series of headaches for the Royal Navy and in particular for the First Sea Lord, Admiral Sir Dudley Pound, who had called the task "a millstone round our necks".

First, the requirement had come at a time when the demand for escort vessels in the Atlantic and for every sort of warship in the Mediterranean were both at a peak. Second, most of the voyage to any of the Russian ports lay within the radius of action of the Luftwaffe squadrons—recently heavily reinforced—based in Norway and Finland, and of a dozen U-boats, which, painted Arctic White and fitted with heaters to keep the vents and the periscopes clear of ice, had been transferred from the Atlantic to strengthen the Soviet blockade. Third, Ultra decodings of German signals traffic indicated that the 50,000-ton *Tirpitz*—the most formidable battleship in the western hemisphere—with the pocket battleships *Admiral Scheer* and *Lützow*, the heavy cruiser *Admiral Hipper* and a number of destroyers, had left their German harbours and were lying, "a fleet in being", in the Trondheim Fiord and Narvik on the north coast of Norway.

Although the voyages in winter were hazardous and arduous, struggling through ice floes, fog and snow-storms, with foot-thick coats of ice building up on every deck and every piece of tackle above

below: A convoy
heading for Britain, as
viewed from an
escorting Royal Navy
destroyer.

the water line, at least the long hours of darkness offered some concealment that the summer months did not. Escorting convoy PQ15 in early May had already cost the Royal Navy two heavy cruisers, *Edinburgh* and *Trinidad*, and the Admiralty had asked the Government to defer more sailings, preferably for ever but at least until the autumn months.

Winston Churchill, however, had promised Marshal Stalin that every effort would be made to get the convoys through, and he remained undeterred by the fact that the Russians showed a total lack of gratitude for all that had been done, but merely called for more and greater sacrifice to match their own appalling losses on the land. All

Churchill cared about was vanquishing the Nazis, and anyone who fought them was his friend. "If Hitler invaded Hell," he had stated, "I would make at least a favourable reference to the Devil in the House of Commons." The Prime Minister had decided that the Russians must be helped, no matter what, and President Roosevelt agreed.

On 27th June 1942 thirty-six merchant ships of four different nationalities, over half of them American, heavily laden with tanks, guns, aeroplanes and trucks, were being marshalled off Reykjavik for the long voyage east. The route lay north-east past Jan Meyen Island, turning east to pass between Bear Island to the south and Spitzbergen to the north, and south-east across the Barents Sea to

Murmansk on the Kola Peninsula. The convoy was designated PQ17.

The close escort group, under Commander Jack Broome, comprised six destroyers, including his own HMS *Keppel*, with four corvettes, three mine-sweepers acting in an anti-submarine role, two anti-aircraft ships, four rescue trawlers and two submarines. The Royal and United States Navies provided a covering force under the command of the British Admiral "Turtle" Hamilton, consisting of his flagship HMS *London*, with the British cruiser *Norfolk* and the USS *Wichita* and *Tuscaloosa* from America, two USN destroyers and seven RN destroyers or corvettes. The Home Fleet's contribution was to be the massive presence,

somewhere to the north-east of the convoy's route, of Admiral Sir John Tovey's flagship *Duke of York*, the British aircraft carrier *Victorious*, the USS *Washington*, flying Admiral Giffen's flag, two cruisers and a mixed bag of fourteen destroyers and corvettes.

Although the merchant ships' ammunition ration had been doubled since the last winter runs, their deck armament was limited and woefully inadequate for a real sea fight. Nevertheless, with a level of protection of almost one to one, there seemed to be a good chance of PQ17 getting through—even if the German big ships intervened.

The pre-sailing conference between the escorts and the merchantmen took place at Hvalfiord, the Royal Navy base in Iceland, on the morning of 27th June. There was little time for more than the usual exhortations to maintain station, to eliminate tell-tale floating debris, and keep stack smoke to a minimum (the sight or smell of smoke, drifting far across the water, had sometimes been the first intimation to the deck-watch on a questing U-boat that a convoy was to windward). One humourist, Commander Broome remembered, overturned the usual warning about the extreme importance of a blackout by advising against showing any sort of darkness in the constant Arctic daylight. One piece of news was that Murmansk had been recently devastated by Luftwaffe bombers and that their new destination was Archangel on the Russian White Sea coast—five hundred miles further from their departure point.

That same day Admiral Tovey received a long signal from the Admiralty, which was obviously intended to cover every imaginable eventuality. The signal's first paragraph deprived him of operational control and, as it transpired, doomed PQ17 before a ship had sailed: "As Admiralty may be in possession of fuller and earlier information of movements of enemy surface forces than our forces will be, and as you may not wish to break W/T silence, it appears necessary for Admiralty to control movements of the convoy

Mystery magnifies danger as the fog the sun.
—Charles Caleb Colton

We have taken the opportunity afforded by the consideration of the report of Mr Harry Hopkins on his return from Moscow to consult together as to how best our two countries can help your country in the splendid defence that you are making against the Nazi attack. We are at the moment co-operating to provide you with the very maximum of supplies that you most urgently need. Already many shiploads have left our shores and more will leave in the immediate future.
—from the "Message to Stalin" speech by Winston S. Churchill, 15th August 1941

right: *Convoy Air Cover*
by Norman Wilkinson.

as far as this may be influenced by movements of enemy surface forces."

On the first day out of Reykjavik, two of the cargo freighters and a tanker, damaged by ice or by running onto rocks around the Icelandic coast, had to return or be assisted back to port. The remaining thirty-three merchant ships, with three rescue ships, four armed trawlers and a substitute tanker, closely shepherded by Commander Broome's escort and spreading across twenty-five square miles of the Arctic Ocean like a floating township, made their progress in orderly columns to the east. Navigation was entirely by dead reckoning, although guesswork might have been an apter word. Magnetic compasses were simply unreliable beyond longitude seventy degrees north, and in the bright, luminous fog that tended to accumulate when the sun shone on the ice, there was little difference between noon, dawn and twilight (as one U-boat man remembered "You lost all sense of time"), and the sun was so low and diffuse on the horizon that there was seldom any chance of taking a sextant shot to establish a position line.

From the fourth day onward, convoy PQ17 was shadowed by a relay of three-engined Blohm-and-Voss 138 reconnaissance aircraft, and shortly after their first appearance a number of U-boats were sighted by the escort and quickly driven off. "Dönitz's second eleven", commented Broome, who had been accustomed to more determined efforts by the North Atlantic wolfpacks. The fact was that both Ubootwaffe headquarters and the U-boat commanders who had been shadowing the convoy since it passed Jan Meyen Island were in some confusion: the Luftwaffe reconnaissance crews had identified the American cruisers *Wichita* and *Tuscaloosa* as aircraft carriers and the British cruiser *London* as a battleship. Furthermore, a westbound convoy, QP13, was in the same vicinity, when only PQ17 had been expected. It was decided that the U-boats should regroup to the east, and let

150

Norman Wilkinson

Shh! Don't talk too much.
Shh! Don't know too much.
Jack, don't be too hip,
'Cause a slip of the lip
Might sink a ship.
—unattributed

The worse the passage the
more welcome the port.
—Thomas Fuller

the Luftwaffe torpedo-bombers have a chance.

Coded signals, meanwhile, flashed across the oceans: course changes, the latest news of pack-ice, orders to the cruiser force to go no further than 25 degrees east, closely followed by another order authorizing it to do so, and, importantly, an air reconnaissance report: "Photographs of Trondheim show that *Tirpitz*, *Hipper* and four destroyers have left." *Tirpitz*, in fact, had moved to Altenfiord and was lying at anchor there, *Lutzow* had run aground, and three of the destroyer screen had been accidentally beached and would be out of action for a while. *Tirpitz*'s

Captain was under orders not to run the slightest risk of tangling with the Home Fleet's carrier-borne aircraft, wherever they might be, without Hitler's personal permission. Back in London, however, the Admiralty were unaware of that: for all Admiral Pound knew on 4th July, at least three heavy surface ships and their destroyers were at sea and closing on PQ17.

Early that morning, while the crews of the US Navy ships kept faith with their forefathers by flying the Stars and Stripes and holding such celebrations as they could, a Heinkel 111 bomber appeared out of the fog and torpedoed the

American Liberty ship *Christopher Newport*. Forty-seven survivors were picked up by a rescue ship, and one of Broome's submarines dispatched the hulk. In the late afternoon six more Heinkels were dissuaded from pressing their attacks home by fierce anti-aircraft fire, but some two hours later a force of twenty-five Focke-Wulfs, flying in from the west, succeeded in torpedoing and stopping three freighters, which were then sunk by gunfire from the escorts to make sure that their cargoes could not be recovered by the enemy. The formation leader made a brave run at low level, avoiding the balloon barrage flown by the merchantmen, and flew straight across the centre of the convoy to torpedo the tanker *Aldersdale*; riddled by gunfire, his burning aircraft crashed into the sea just ahead of *Keppel* in the lead.

Three more torpedo-bombers were claimed by the escort's guns, and Broome was heartened by the knowledge that with every passing hour the convoy was moving further away from the Heinkels' bases on the north Norwegian coast. He made an entry in his log: "My impression of seeing the resolution displayed by the convoy and its escort was that, provided the ammunition lasted, PQ17 could get anywhere." It was an opinion that even on later reflection he saw no cause to alter.

That night more signals came from London, one after another. The first, from the First Sea Lord himself, ordered Admiral Hamilton's cruiser force, at that point steaming a few miles to the north and forward of the convoy, to withdraw westward at full speed. The next, minutes later, instructed the convoy to disperse and proceed to Russian ports "owing to threat from surface ships". Along with many sailors of all ranks in the close escort, Broome found the import of the order difficult to credit. Was there not always a threat from surface ships in hostile seas? Was that not what they were there to meet? But if that last signal had not been enough to ensure the fate of PQ17, the next, classified "Secret" and graded "Most Immediate",

read "Convoy is to scatter" and made it absolutely certain. The signal's implication was that the threat was so menacing and immediate that the ships of the convoy would stand more chance of survival if they broke ranks and spread in all directions.

It was at this point that Broome, on the bridge of *Keppel*, saw Hamilton's cruisers turning back to westward and putting on speed. To him at that moment, unaware as he was of their orders from London, they had the look of ships going into battle. If they were going to fight *Tirpitz*, *Scheer* and *Hipper*, with their destroyer screen, which he assumed must be closing on the convoy, it was his duty to give all assistance. In turmoil, but bound by that belief, he sent this signal to the convoy skippers: "Scatter fanwise and proceed at your utmost speed."

Broome sent one last, apologetic message to the convoy Commodore in *River Afton* and received a courteous reply. He turned his destroyers westward to link with the cruiser force, instructing the remainder of the close escort group to make for Archangel and to give the merchant ships whatever help they could. Referring to the Admiralty's last order, Broome later wrote that it "had to be obeyed or ignored. To my dying regret I obeyed it." Admiral Hamilton, for his part, made a signal to his cruiser Captains: "I know you will be as distressed as I am to leave that fine collection of ships to find their own way to harbour."

Between them, in the next five days, first the Luftwaffe and then the U-boats, plying from Kirkenes west of Murmansk, and acting more as scavengers than wolfpacks, sent an oiler, a rescue ship and nineteen freighters to the bottom of the Barents Sea. A few antiquated Russian aircraft appeared above the shambles and, more from force of habit than from need, the more wary U-boat commanders took a dive, only to resurface and seek another prey when the aircraft flew away. It was, as Captain Samuel E. Morison recorded in his history of the times, "a via doloroso for every

The ugliest of trades have their moments of pleasure. Now, if I were a gravedigger, or even a hangman, there are some people I could work for with a great deal of enjoyment.
—from *Ugly Trades* by Douglas Jerrold

The tide was now set and running strongly against all Allied shipping...It was like a dark stain spreading all over the huge sea; the area of safety diminished, the poisoned water, in which no ship could count on safety from hour to hour, seemed swiftly to infect a wider and wider circle...
—from *The Cruel Sea* by Nicholas Montserrat

left: A mountain of water erupts with the explosion of depth-charges from the US Coast Guard cutter *Spencer*, commanded by Harold Berdine, as she attacks *U-175*, commanded by Gerhardt Muntz. Muntz was about to attack a vessel in convoy HX-233 when the *Spencer*, one of the convoy escorts, found the U-boat by the use of sonar.

merchant ship". Eleven ships, most of them heavily laden with frostbitten survivors pulled from the icy waters, at last limped into port, some after taking refuge for weeks among the icebergs north of Archangel, with their stacks and superstructures camouflaged white, thanks to the Arctic experience of one of the freighter skippers.

Down with the total toll of twenty-two sunken vessels, evenly shared between the aircraft and the U-boats, went 123,000 tons of war supplies for Russia, including 210 out of 297 aircraft, 430 out of 594 tanks, and 3,350 out of 4,246 vehicles. One hundred and fifty-three men had died, with many more maimed or frostbitten. One group rowed a life-boat for ten days only to find they had landed in occupied Norway, where they were promptly made prisoners of war.

The voyage of PQ17 was over; *Tirpitz* had changed one anchorage for another, and someone in London—maybe everyone in London—had misread the signs. Stalin, typically, asked if the Royal Navy had any sense of glory. Justifications, recriminations and debate would go on for many years. It was, as Winston Churchill said, "one of the most melancholy episodes in the whole of the war". The next Russian convoy did not sail until September, when twelve merchantmen went down, but at a cost to Germany of three U-boats and twenty-two torpedo-bombers. After the return trip there was a change of plan: no more big ships would sail on the Russian run, but destroyers, trawlers and corvettes would escort the convoys all the way, and, as resistance in the air and on the water weakened, more and more got through.

As for the great ship *Tirpitz*, she remained a threat in northern waters until 12th November 1944, when, after many brave attempts to sink her by the Royal Navy, the Fleet Air Arm and Bomber Command, thirty-two Lancasters of Nos 9 and 617 Squadrons found her in the Tromsöe Fiord, scored two direct hits with 12,000-pound "Tallboy" bombs and sent her to the bottom with a thousand of her crew.

No British merchant ship was ever held in port by its crew, even at the height of the Battle of the Atlantic, when to cross that ocean in a slow-moving merchant ship was to walk hand in hand with death for every minute of the day and night. Nor, when there was a need to supply arms to the Soviet Union via the Arctic route, did they flinch. German surface ships and aircraft, based in northern Norway, savaged them without mercy, while the ever-present U-boats continued to snap at their heels like the Hounds of Hell. Of those who died— and they were legion—the fortunate fell to the guns and torpedoes of the enemy, the luckless froze to death in minutes in the icy waters of the Arctic Sea. Those who were spared to reach their goals often endured round-the-clock bombing by German aircraft while in port. But the greatest indignity many of these men suffered was to be treated by their erstwhile Soviet allies as outcasts, tainted by the dread disease of capitalism.
—from *The Merchant Navy Goes To War* by Bernard Edwards

left: *The U-309 on Atlantic patrol*, by John Hamilton. overleaf: Ice on a Type IIB boat in the north Atlantic.

It's getting to be a different kind of war, Number One, and the people in it have got different too. In the beginning there was time for all sorts of things...understanding people, making allowances for them, wondering whether they were happy...even whether they liked you or not. Now, the war doesn't seem to be a matter of feelings anymore. Now it's just a matter of killing the enemy.
—from *The Cruel Sea* by Nicholas Montserrat

I was much further out
than you thought / And
not waving but drowning.
—from *Selected Poems*
by Stevie Smith

WHEN THE CREW of a U-boat, so smart, neatly shaved and barbered on the day they set out, returned to the harbour from patrol and stood roughly at attention in two rows along the decks as the boat was moored against the quay, they bore a resemblance to the less presentable elements of Attila's hordes and probably smelt worse. From the Commander down to the humblest hand they were dirty, haggard, shabby and unkempt. The only men with neither beards nor stubble were those who were too young to develop facial hair in the passage of six weeks. It was only the happy gleam in their eyes that showed just how they felt about being where they were—back from that small, dim world below the sea.

Their attire made a striking contrast with the well-tailored uniforms, the gleaming shoes and buttons, the healthy, beaming faces of the welcoming party that assembled on the quayside—the Flotilla Commander with members of his staff, representatives of the Flag Officer U-boats West and the BdU, of the Army garrison and the shipyard administration, members of the Women's Naval Auxiliary, nurses from the hospital and, a little way apart, the bright dresses, shining hair and smiling lips of the ladies of the town.

Throughout the last few days of the return voyage there had been little relaxation. Apart from the ever-present danger of attack and the need for constant vigilance there had been a mass of paper-work: the writing up of the *Kriegstagebuch* (the Commander's war diary), requisition forms for stores, lists of items for replacement and/or repair, signals logs, leave applications and everything in triplicate, quadruplicate or more. The crew had remembered to remove the bedding blankets from where they had been airing on the jumping wire and to fly a victory pennant for each ship they had sunk.

Now, for a while, they could escape the narrow confines of the boat and rejoin the human race. It was like being born again, to emerge from the darkness into light. Once they had regained their land-legs, and enjoyed the luxury of a real, hot bath, a haircut and a shave, there would be a splendid, formal dinner, with congratulatory patriotic speeches, plenty of French wine or German beer, or both, and the best of food. What they most looked forward to, however, was reading the accumulated mail from home.

Then, while the boat was in the bunker, and always subject to operational requirements, they might expect a few weeks' respite from the perils of the sea. For this, they might take turns on a roster: a third of the crew on leave at home, a third "out to pasture" in one of the rest camps, while the last third were servicing and cleaning up the boat. The men going on leave could buy rare goodies for the folk back home from special seamen's shops, then travel on one of the official stores trains that

Lovers in peace-time / With fifty years to live, / Have time to tease and quarrel / And question what to give; / But lovers in war-time Better understand. / The fullness of living, / With death close at hand.
—from *The White Cliffs* by Alice Duer Miller

far left: U-boat captain Adelbert Schnee is welcomed ashore at the port of Saint-Nazaire in 1942, feeling extremely rubber-kneed after many weeks at sea on a swaying submarine. left: Kapitänleutnant Joachim Schepke celebrates his return from a patrol in September 1940.

O Captain! my captain!
our fearful trip is done; /
The ship has weathered
every rack; the prize we
sought is won.
—Walt Whitman

right: Crewmembers of *U-29*, a Type VIIA boat, enjoy a meal on deck while moored at Brest in October 1940. above: An image of Brest in 1996.

made regular runs between the west of France and northern Germany.

Although the official rest and recuperation centres had facilities for sport and entertainment and were normally immune from Allied bombs, many of the crewmen preferred to spend their hours of liberty in places of their choice—in the sort of places where women, wine and food—in whatever their order of priority—were readily available. In pursuing this requirement, it was one advantage of a U-boat sailor's life that while he was at sea there was nothing for him to spend his money on, and on return to port his accumulated back-pay was enough to satisfy his every whim. If his main need were for female company, there was plenty to be had, and although the flotilla staff, who lived their lives at some distance from the dark Atlantic depths, always seemed to have the pick of it (for the front line men it was ever thus), there were the German nurses, clerks and typists who worked at the headquarters, and the U-boat hostel staff; furthermore, there were plenty of young local Frenchwomen who, unlike their counterparts in Britain, were not required to join the services, till the land or "do their bit" in the munitions factories.

When all else failed, there were always the local professionals, but the U-boat men were warned that some of these *mademoiselles* were involved with the Resistance and that they must at all times guard their tongues. The slightest remark about personnel, duties, equipment, movements, even hopes and expectations, might get back to ears in London.

At Lorient—"the ace of bases"—the people of Brittany did not seem unfriendly to the U-boat crews, who treated them with equivalent amity, tinged with a certain nuance of contempt. Germany was far away, as indeed was Paris. Shore patrols and Military Police maintained a watchful presence and were as unpopular as always, but at least no cold-eyed Gestapo agents prowled the streets.

At Brest, a pleasant if somewhat dilapidated town about sixty miles to the northwest, pens were

160

far left: U-boat men dance and drink at a lounge in France in the summer of 1942, centre: a gun port in the U-bunker at La Pallice, left: The old town centre, La Rochelle, below: The harbour from the old lock, La Pallice.

The bee that hath honey in her mouth hath a sting in her tail.
—from *Euphues*
by John Lyly

available for fifty U-boats of the resident flotillas, with accommodation for the staff and the sea-going officers in the Hotel Beau Séjour, a fine four-storey building in the market place. The erstwhile French Prefecture and the palatial naval college served as an operational headquarters and an officers' mess. For entertainment, the Petty Officers and ratings enjoyed the amenities of the Pigeon Blanc, among many other welcoming establishments. One of the most popular was the Casino Bar, where while all drank their fill, the handsome, dark-haired Madame could be persuaded to turn off the gramophone and put on a movie calculated to stimulate her patrons' interest in her company of girls—girls of different colours, shapes and sizes, but alike in their readiness to please. (Allied bomber crews returning to their rural bases in the east of England seldom, if ever, enjoyed a similar reception.)

It was common for the U-boat men (and also for the fliers), when they were at liberty and enjoying themselves, to establish a rapport with others of their calling and arrange to meet again. The sadness came when, returning from their next patrol or flight, they discovered that their new-found friends had not come back from theirs. It was at such times that a man might well decide it would be less traumatic to confine his friendships to those who sailed or flew with him; that way, if they went down, the chances were that he would go down too.

A leave spent at home in the German countryside, or in a town untroubled by the Allied bombers, was always the best sort of rest and recuperation; the only difficulty was that loving parents dearly wanted to show off their brave boy, in his uniform and medals, to all their acquaintances and friends, while all he wanted was to put the U-boats and the war out of his mind. Even so, such homecomings were probably less traumatic than a leave spent in a city that had suffered heavy air attacks and lay under the threat of more.

There the seaman would find the streets full of debris, shattered glass and metal, and millions of strips of the metal foil that was dropped from the bombers to overwhelm the radar; buildings he knew well would be lying naked and stripped of walls and roofs, with the stench of smoke and burned cordite everywhere, and many thousands of people whose homes had been destroyed would be seeking sustenance and shelter. He might find that his wife, his fiancée, or members of his family, were tense, dispirited and nervous—almost different people from those he loved and had longed to see—worse than that, they might be among the dead or injured. Many a seaman, having spent most of his leave among the frightened people in an air-raid shelter, felt he would rather be at sea.

As a result Paris, German-occupied but immune from bombing, became a magnet for the U-boat men on leave, just as London—although by no means immune from bombs, "doodlebugs" and rockets—attracted Allied airmen based in Britain.

Herbert Werner, a U-boat 1st Officer, and later commander, who sailed on ten missions and spent a year of days at sea, described his experiences in his excellent book *Iron Coffins*. His home was in bomb-torn Frankfurt, but in 1943 he found that the French capital provided the restful atmosphere needed on breaks from his duties aboard *U-230*. "I wished to forget", he wrote, "that I was a cog in the war machine...only one place seemed to transmit the sense of freedom and tranquility I desired—Paris. It did not disappoint me; I felt the city's spell as people of many nations had felt it...I was entirely divorced from the war for twelve pure hours." Later, in Frankfurt, Werner observed the contrast with the atmosphere of Paris: "It was an irony that Frenchmen, having lost the war, ate like kings while we, the victors, lived on potatoes and ersatz."

As the war dragged on into its fourth year, with the news from the eastern, the western and the southern fronts equally bad, there were few happy faces on the jetty to meet the U-boats when they returned to port, the home-coming dinner parties

On their first night ashore the crew dined as usual with Kretschmer at Beau Séjour, and after the toasts—a few more than usual, to celebrate their success—they were told that a rest camp had been provided for them near Lorient at Quiberon, where all facilities were available for sports and entertainment. They were to be taken there for a week the next day.
—from *The Golden Horseshoe*
by Terence Robertson

It is only the first bottle that is expensive.
—French proverb

Brandy is lead in the morning, silver at noon, gold at night.
—German proverb

left: Kapitänleutnant Erich Topp, commander of *U-552* greeted warmly on his return to his French port from a patrol 19th June 1942.

fell short of merriment, and exchanges of "Zum Wohl!" and "Prosit!" were less hearty than before. There were more empty places at the messhall tables, and the local girls, once so compliant and amenable, but now wary of how they would be treated when France was liberated, now kept their distance. And when a U-boat left its base to go to

war, there were few well-wishers on the waterfront, no brass bands or flowers. Nevertheless, the war went on, and Doctor Göbbels's broadcasts sought to cheer the fighting seamen with the news that formidable new war-winning weapons would soon be launched against the British and, in due course, the Americans.

All too quickly the time ashore was over. The long, grey U-boat lay floating in its bunker, repaired, repainted and cleaned, crammed with torpedoes, fuel, food and ammunition and ready to take them on another long and perilous journey. As they humped their kit aboard, they hoped grimly that she would also bring them home.

left: Kapitänleutnant Hoffmann, of *U-447*, with his wife and child. below left: *U-95* at Saint-Nazaire in March 1941. below: A smart military band salutes *U-29* as she sets out from Lorient in 1940.

ON 11TH MARCH 1940 Squadron Leader Delap of No.82 Squadron, RAF Bomber Command, piloting a twin-engined Bristol Blenheim, attacked a surfaced U-boat at low level in the Schillig Roads near Wilhelmshaven in the Heligoland Bight. The U-boat, *U-31*, was hit by Delap's bombs and sank off Borkum Island. Although on that occasion she was salvaged and repaired (only to be sent down—permanently—in the Atlantic eight months later by the destroyer *Antelope*), *U-31* must stand as the first U-boat to be sunk by air attack in World War II. *U-320*, bombed by a Consolidated PBY Catalina of Coastal Command almost five years later, was the 196th and the last to meet death from the sky.

From the first years of the war, the RAF's heavy bombers, joined in 1942 by those of the USAAF, frequently attacked the shipyards and U-boat bases at Kiel, Hamburg, Wilhelmshaven and Bremen on the Baltic coast, and they continued to do so until Germany surrendered. Thousands of mines were laid in the approaches to the bases, and U-boats, setting out on patrol or returning home, had to be shepherded by trawlers or patrol boats through the dangerous waters. As the war progressed, U-boats at sea were increasingly harried by aircraft of the Allied maritime commands.

The RAF's Fleet Air Arm had been handed over to the Royal Navy in 1938, and in December 1940, after much heart-searching, the Air Ministry had moreover decided that, although it would retain ownership and the administration of Coastal Command, operational control would pass to the Admiralty on 1st April 1941. The decision was unexceptionable, and in reaching it the Air Marshals showed a better understanding of inter-service relations than was ever exhibited by Reichsmarschall Hermann Göring, whose philosophy was illustrated by his phrase: "Anything that flies belongs to me, and me alone." In practice, however, the British plan did not quite work out—at least not for some time. The Coastal Commander-in-Chief, Air Chief Marshal Sir Philip Joubert, described it

as "a polite fiction", and in September 1942 he called for "a single supreme control for the whole anti-U-boat campaign to co-ordinate the policies of British, Canadian and American naval and air authorities". Although it was generally agreed that such a policy was strategically desirable, if not to say essential, it was politically impossible: the post of anti-submarine Supremo was certain to fall to a British Admiral, and neither President Roosevelt, nor any good American, could go along with that.

For most of the war Coastal Command was to remain the RAF's Cinderella force: Fighter and Bomber Commands had more glamour, more apparent action and a higher priority with the aircraft and armaments industries. So it was that, in the early days, with the planes available, the Coastal crews' duties lay mainly in reconnaissance—patrolling the sea-lanes in search of the enemy and radioing any sightings to the Navy. Of the Command's seventeen squadrons, the majority were equipped with the twin-engined Avro Anson, dating from the early 1930s, a lovely aeroplane to fly, but slow, limited in range, and woefully short of fire-power. Only three squadrons had the sort of aircraft—the Short Sunderland and the American Lockheed Hudson—capable of patrolling the far Atlantic waters and, with their depth charges and machine guns, of taking the offensive against a U-boat if they should ever find one.

At least these aircraft were effective in their role. In a scrap with eight Junkers 88s, a Sunderland's gunners shot three of the enemy planes down, and the big flying boat was thereafter known by German pilots as "the flying porcupine". A Hudson of 269 Squadron on patrol from Iceland on 27th August 1941, attacked *U-570* with such effect that the commander, Kapitänleutnant Rahmlow, submerging in a hurry, neglected to close all the vents and hatches. The flooded batteries produced a cloud of chlorine gas, the boat promptly surfaced and a dozen choking crewmen struggled from the conning tower on to the deck. In the words of the Hudson pilot: "We thought at first they were making

MORS AB ALTO

After pulling out of the dive and around in position to see the submarine, it appeared to be settling straight down, until suddenly from the conning tower forward, it shot up in the air, and then there was a terrific cone-shaped explosion coming from and surrounding the entire sub, which rose high in the air. As this subsided, everything seemed to be swallowed by the sea.
—Lieutenant Samuel K. Taylor, from his official report of an action in which his Liberator bomber sank a U-boat in early January 1944.

left: *U-848* under attack by four PB4Ys and two B-25s on 5th November 1943 in the south Atlantic off Ascencion Island. The U-boat, a Type IXD2, was sunk by the attacking aircraft.

Man goeth to his long home.
—Old Testament, Ecclesiastes, XII, 5

for their guns, so we kept our own guns going hard. They didn't like that a bit, and tried to scamble back again. The rest of the crew were trying to get out of the hatch, and they sort of met in the middle and argued it out. It was a regular shambles for a few minutes."

The pilot made low, tight turns around the U-boat, with his guns trained on the conning tower, and a piece of white material, which turned out to be the commander's starched dress shirt, was waved in surrender. The Hudson's fuel was running low, and the wireless operator signalled for assistance, while the pilot circled. "Practically the whole crew", he reported, "seemed to be in the conning tower, packed in so tightly they could hardly move. We were close enough to see their faces, and a glummer-looking lot I never saw in my life." A relay of aircraft kept watch over the prize until a destoyer arrived to escort her into port—the first U-boat to be captured intact. She was towed to

Iceland, repaired, and later served the Royal Navy as HMS *Graph*. *U-570*'s flag was presented to 269 Squadron by the Navy as a memento of the feat. Her 1st Officer, Bernhardt Berndt, was condemned as a coward by his fellow Ubootwaffe POWs and, in an attempt to redeem his honour by escaping (with the aim of scuttling his captured U-boat at Barrow-in-Furness) was shot dead by a patrol of "Dad's Army"—Britain's Home Guard. Post-war, the unhappy Rahmlow was denied membership of the U-boat Old Comrades' Association, and it is notable that in Admiral Dönitz's memoirs, which contain some reference to almost every U-boat that came under his command, the fate of *U-570* is not mentioned.

Meanwhile, the many hundreds of thousands of licensed private pilots in America had found themselves a role in national defence. On 1st

"I guess that means those Yank-built Consolidated 'Catalina' flyingboats or maybe those big four engined British Short 'Sunderland' flyingboats," Dave added in a speculative manner. "Well, either one suits me. Both are tip-top crates. But that means patrolling over coastal waters hunting for submarines. Heck, unless the bus falls apart and you drop into the drink I can't see much danger in that kind of work."
—from *Dave Dawson on Convoy Patrol* by R. Sidney Bowen

far left: A beautifully restored Consolidated PBY Catalina flying boat at the San Diego Aerospace Museum. left: HMS *Pursuer*, a British escort carrier whose Grumman Wildcat fighters successfully defended a valuable convoy in a night action against Heinkel and Focke-Wulf aircraft 380 miles west of Cape Finisterre in 1944.

December 1941, six days before the Japanese attack on the US Navy's big ships in Pearl Harbor, they had formed the Civil Air Patrol. In the best tradition of the Minutemen of the War of Independence, they stood by at airfields in every eastern state, ready to fly to America's defence at a minute's notice. Once General Arnold was convinced of their potential, the Air Corps provided them with fuel, and Washington, somewhat grudgingly, paid the pilots $8 per day ($5 for the ground staff), out

of which they had to find their own uniforms, servicing, food and accommodation.

Their service gave no exemption from the draft, and as time went on most of the younger men and women joined the armed forces, but their elders always filled the gaps. In their miscellaneous collection of red-and-yellow Stinsons, Fairchilds, Taylorcraft and Wacos, always flying in pairs, they patrolled the eastern seaboard at low level, up to sixty miles offshore, from dawn to dusk. They had single-channel radios, and their life-jackets were the inner tubes of motor tyres.

When the CAP flights had proved their worth by sighting U-boats, ships in distress and drifting lifeboats, and reporting their positions, the big oil companies combined to make a hefty grant of cash, and the Air Corps provided 100-pound bombs and 350-pound depth-charges to be carried under the patrolling aircrafts' wings. In July 1942 a Widgeon thus equipped, flying out of Atlantic City, was the

far left: Grumman Avengers attacking a U-boat. below: An RAF Lockheed Hudson bomber with its crew.

first to attack and claim the sinking of a U-boat, twenty-five miles off the coast of New Jersey. In the eighteen months before the US Navy took over all anti-U-boat warfare and confined the CAP to search-and-rescue missions, the flying Minutemen flew 86,685 sorties, made 173 U-boat sightings, dropped 82 bombs or depth-charges and claimed the destruction or damage of two U-boats. They lost 90 aircraft and 26 fliers. The Navy's Commander, Admiral King, recorded his appreciation of their "valuable contributions", and his staff, eschewing all effusiveness, noted their "interesting record of service".

In the final months of 1941, the Italian ships tasked with keeping Feldmarshall Rommel's Africa Corps in Libya supplied were taking heavy punishment from Royal Navy warships and Fleet Air Arm fighters flying off the carrier *Ark Royal*. In an effort to assist his axis partner, Hitler ordered Dönitz to transfer the bulk of the Atlantic U-boat force to the Mediterranean and the Straits of Gibraltar. Mussolini would provide a base at La Spezia, on the north-west coast of Italy. Not only was Dönitz dismayed at the effect of this deployment on his Atlantic strategy, but he also realized how tricky the task of his crews in the Mediterranean would be. The U-boats could be spotted by an aircraft through the clear blue waters even when they were submerged at sixty metres. It was a case of surfacing, launching torpedoes and quickly diving low again, with no chance of observing the results.

Nevertheless, the U-boats made an impact on the North African campaign. Within a month *Ark Royal* had been torpedoed by *U-81* and sunk before she could be towed into Gibraltar, *U-331* had dispatched the 31,000-ton HMS *Barham* (the only battleship ever sunk on the high seas by the Ubootwaffe), and *U-557* had sent down the cruiser *Galatea*. The loss of *Ark Royal*'s air striking power against the Africa Corps' supply lines was a major blow and contributed to the fact that, by January 1942, Rommel's divisions were moving east again. Meanwhile, the Atlantic convoys enjoyed a

There can be three or four U-boats in a 20,000 mile area that you are patrolling constantly and you may never see them. If they happen to be lucky and pop up to recharge their battery five minutes after your plane has flown over them, they probably have two hours during which they can remain surfaced safely. The only way you can guarantee that there are no U-boats in an area like that is to keep every square mile of it under continuous surveillance for about thirty-six hours. By that time any sub in the area would be forced to come up and recharge its battery. But a jeep carrier task group cannot keep the whole area covered all the time. Actually, at any given instant our four night-flying turkeys would have about six per cent of our total area on their radar scopes. By sweeping this six per cent back and forth at 150 knots for four hours, we stood a good chance of finding any U-boat that surfaced for as long as an hour, but we couldn't be sure of doing it.
—from *Twenty Million Tons Under The Sea* by Rear Admiral Daniel V. Gallery, USN

left: *Sunderland Attacking a Wolfpack* by Norman Wilkinson.

brief and welcome respite.

For the airmen serving in an anti-submarine role one highly frustrating feature was that their achievements were often impossible to assess, as was described in the official pamphlet *Coastal Command* published by His Majesty's Stationery Office in 1942: "The attack is so swift and the results, if any, so prompt that the surface of the sea has closed like a curtain too swiftly for them to be accurately perceived and recorded. Though great patches of oil have stained the sea, though bubbles have formed and burst upon it, the U-boat may not be stricken to death. It may still be able to limp back to one of the numerous bases at its disposal for a refuge between the North of Norway and the South-West of France. On the other hand, it is equally possible that the opposite may have occurred and that the bombs or depth-charges have accomplished their purpose and that the U-boat went down on the long slant to destruction, manned by a crew of choked and drowning men."

Following the Sunderlands and Hudsons came the long-range American PBYs—equipped with British radar and bomb-racks—together with some mid-range fighter-bombers, such as the Bristol Blenheim and the Beaufighter, and the longer-range Vickers Wellington, a twin-engined bomber that was being replaced in Air Chief Marshal Harris's Command by four-engined heavies. The weapons also—new 300-pound depth-charges, 600-pound bombs, torpedoes with acoustic homers and new low-level bombsights, were far more effective, and the mere sight of an aircraft turning to attack was enough to force a U-boat to submerge and so be diverted from its prey.

Most important was the latest electronic aid—centimetric radar—forty precious sets of which, recently acquired by his Command, the British bomber chief had been persuaded to transfer to the Coastal Command Wellingtons. Seated in his cabin at 10,000 feet, the radar operator could scan nearly 4,000 square miles of sea, and a "blip"

painted on his screen by the rotating antenna showed him the range and bearing of its source. The effect was immediate, and it came as an unpleasant shock to the watch on a U-boat's bridge to see an aircraft not merely searching but heading straight towards them from over the horizon and sometimes out of heavy cloud. If an airborne radar was directed at them, they expected warning from the "Metox" detector, but this proved ineffective against short-wave transmissions of the new search radars. Many a radio report to BdU read: "Crash dive. Attack by aircraft. No radar warning."

If his U-boat were one of those equipped with more and better anti-aircraft armament, a

previous spread: Captured crewmen of *U-175* taken aboard the US Coast Guard cutter *Spencer*, which had just sunk their boat using depth-charges. left: nineteen members of the crew of *U-175* were rescued by the *Spencer* and a further twenty-two were picked up by the cutter *Duane*.

HOLDING THE LINE!

...we gave orders to the R.A.F. Coastal Command to dominate the outlets from the Mersey and Clyde and around Northern Ireland. Nothing must be spared from this task. It had supreme priority. The bombing of Germany took second place. All suitable machines, pilots, and material must be concentrated upon our counter-offensive, by fighters against the enemy bombers, and surface craft assisted by bombers against the U-boats in these narrow vital waters. Many other important projects were brushed aside, delayed, or mauled. At all costs one must breathe.
—from *The Second World War: Their Finest Hour* by Winston S. Churchill

commander might decide to stay on the surface and fight it out, in which case the pilot could either reciprocate or circle out of range while calling up the nearest corvette or destroyer. If the commander opted to submerge, the aircrew, watching through binoculars, would see the first man disappear into the conning tower, at which they would perhaps have thirty seconds in which to make their attack, with bombs, depth charges or torpedoes; if they were skilled enough and quick enough, they might catch the raider at its most vulnerable time.

Adapting to the threat, the U-boat commanders changed their tactics, staying down longer in the daylight hours and surfacing in darkness to launch their attacks. One of the counter-measures to the night assault was provided by the "Snowflake" rockets, fired by the ships to illuminate the scene; another, more effective one, was the "Leigh" light (named after the RAF Squadron Leader who invented it), installed in two squadrons of Wellingtons in the late summer of 1942 and in the PBYs and B-24s when they joined the anti-submarine campaign. When the aircraft's radar found a surfaced U-boat, the pilot approached it in a shallow dive and switched on the Leigh light at about 150 feet. The brilliant broad beam, focused on the conning tower, turned the night to

day, blinding the deck watch while the aircraft made its bombing run.

In the early years of the war, U-boats on long-range patrol were refuelled at sea by surface tankers, but by the end of 1941 all of these had been hunted down and sunk by the Royal Navy—a fate not entirely unexpected by the Kriegsmarine. In 1942, ten big Type IX U-boats were specially constructed to rearm, resupply and refuel the boats at sea and to carry medical stores and replacements for sick or wounded crewmen. The 1,600-ton "milch cows", as the Royal Navy called them, had a range of over 12,000 nautical miles and a speed of ten knots, and each carried enough diesel oil to double the endurance of five convoy raiders. There was nothing wrong with the conception, but the operational problems were formidable. To effect a rendezvous between two small vessels in the vastness of the ocean called for very skilful navigation; it also took time, while each lay on the surface, readily detectable by radar or by eye, to transfer fuel and supplies and to row or tow torpedoes from one boat to the other. Life-jackets were attached to the fuel pipe to keep it afloat, but it was liable to break if the oil were pumped too fast. The Allied air forces and navies were quick to seize upon the weaknesses and to give the U-tankers their full attention. The original ten were quickly sunk, and ten more planned for 1943 were cancelled when it became clear to BdU that the ever-growing scale of the anti-submarine campaign made the U-tanker not so much a milch cow as a dead duck.

The airmen of Coastal Command had always felt an empathy with the Royal Navy, and they worked closely with their sea-borne comrades in a way that the Luftwaffe, except above the Baltic against the Russian convoys, very seldom did. The only air support available to Admiral Dönitz was supplied by a few Focke-Wulf Condors based at Bordeaux, and the Condor, a converted civil transport plane, had neither the equipment, nor endurance, nor had its crews the experience, for long-range reconnaissance operations. It was in an attempt to improve this situation that Dönitz, overcoming, for the moment, his aversion to the epicurean Reichsmarschall, visited Göring's vast hunting estate on the Lithuanian border and, among the elk, wolves and bison that abounded there, made a plea for more support. The long trip from Lorient brought him the temporary assistance of some twenty-four twin-engined Junkers 88C fighter-bombers to reinforce the Condors.

It was not enough. By the beginning of 1943, the Allies' U-boat hunters were flying from bases in Iceland, Scotland, Northern Ireland, south-west England, Gibraltar, West Africa, Canada and the eastern seaboard of America, and in the early spring the Allies' military successes in North Africa released a number of long-range Consolidated Liberators, each capable of carrying a load of twenty-four 300-pound depth-charges, to close the mid-Atlantic gap. Of forty-one U-boats sunk in May, twenty-three were victims of air attack, and the casualty rate to Dönitz's fleet rose to an insupportable 63 per cent. He complained to Hitler:"It is wholly incomprehensible that the German Navy, in this twentieth century, the century of aircraft, is called upon to fight without an air arm and without air reconnaissance of its own." There was worse to come: in August, an agreement with her oldest ally, Portugal, gave Britain access to two air bases in the Azores, a thousand miles west of Gibraltar in the North Atlantic. Moreover as has been recorded, Air Chief Marshal Harris was occasionally persuaded to lend his heavy hand to the anti-submarine campaign. A new bomber crew, flying their first mission, would often be sent "gardening" (the code word for mine-laying), to plant a row of "vegetables" in the U-boat channels off the Biscay coast. Jack Currie's Lancaster crew, for instance, had their first experience of being fired upon when, searching for the dropping zone off La Pallice, they ventured too close to the guns of La Rochelle. The results of such missions could seldom be assessed, but they were reckoned to

far left: At considerable risk of air attack, *U-107* takes on fuel from a tanker in the south Atlantic in May 1941. left: On 24th May 1943, RAF Whitley pilot Sergeant Clifford Chatten scored a hit on *U-523* forcing it to return to Lorient for repairs.

have caused the Ubootwaffe some inconvenience as they went about their work.

On 21st May 1943 Sergeant Clifford Chatten, piloting a Whitley while still under training, found a surfaced U-boat some 500 miles off the coast of France and attacked it from fifty feet with a stick of five 250-pound depth-charges (the fifth was a "hang-up" and failed to leave the bomb-bay). The attack was just too late: the U-boat disappeared below the surface thirty seconds before the weapons fell.

Three days later, on a similar patrol, Chatten found another target and made his attack from up-sun at 100 feet. This time, all of the depth-charges were released, and the photographs taken by the automatic camera showed that at least one had scored a hit. "It is certain", claimed a subsequent Command Routine Order, "that very severe damage was done. In all probability, the U-boat was sunk."

The claim, as sometimes happened, was not supported by the facts, but *U-523* was damaged and had to return to Lorient for repairs. "If we'd been carrying bombs", Chatten recalls, "I'm sure we would have sunk it." Having completed his OTU course, Chatten was posted to 83 Squadron of the Pathfinder Force and proved to be a fine Lancaster pilot, but it was his record as a submarine hunter that marks him out for history. There were many highly experienced Coastal Command pilots who spent hundreds of hours flying over water and never saw a U-boat, let alone attacked one, while Chatten, the rookie, found and attacked two within four days.

Chatten's unit, No. 10 Operational Training Unit, was exclusively employed for eleven months on anti-submarine patrols. In 1,848 sorties, the embryo crews recorded 91 sightings and made 54 attacks. The results—one "Known Sunk", one "Probably Damaged" and two "Probably Slightly Damaged"—seem a woefully small return for the loss of thirty-three aircraft, but, as the First Sea Lord wrote in a message to the unit, "this constant and strenuous endeavour has very materially added to the

difficulties of the U-boat in passing the Bay [of Biscay] and thus contributed to the subsequent U-boat sightings and sinkings".

On a clear night in June 1944, a few hours after the Normandy invasion had begun, a Liberator on patrol between the Scillies and Ushant found a surfaced U-boat and sank it with a perfect "straddle" of six depth-charges, three on each side of the hull. Twenty-two minutes later, a second dark silhouette appeared against the moonlit water; it was the aircrew's lucky night. Their gunfire was hotly returned from the U-boat's deck, but the attack went on—four depth-charges fell on the port beam and two on the starboard. The U-boat went down by the stern and took a list to starboard. With their bomb load expended, the aircrew watched anxiously.

"We were just going to send a message to base," said the pilot, "hoping someone might come and finish the job, when the mid-upper gunner shouted 'She's going down. It's just like a Hollywood picture.' She was at an angle of 75 degrees, with her bow high in the air, sliding slowly into the sea. We hadn't needed the Leigh light for the attacks, but now we switched it on. It showed three dinghies, with the Germans in them, floating among the debris and oil. It all happened so quickly that the wireless operator, busy sending a report of the first attack to base, didn't realise what was going on, and he thought we were kidding him."

Although the operations of the Allies' maritime air commands and naval air arm did not figure in the headlines as often as those of the bomber and fighter commands, their long-sustained contribution to the Atlantic battle was enormous. Crews of the RAF's Coastal Command flew 800,000 hours above the oceans and made 1,300 attacks on enemy vessels. One thousand seven hundred aeroplanes were lost in those missions, and 5,800 aircrew—including 1,600 from Britain's Dominions and her European allies—lost their lives while flying them.

By January 1943, two things about the antisubmarine bombing program had become clear. In the first place, earlier assumptions regarding the imperforability of the pens were now borne out by experience. Even with the use of heavier armor-piercing ammunition it was considered doubtful whether significant damage could be done to the pen blocks. Consequently, all that could be hoped for from bombing of bases would be disorganization of the turn-around and servicing schedule. Secondly, in order to paralyze the operating bases and so to deny them to the Germans, it would be necessary to employ much larger forces and to bomb much more frequently than had hitherto been feasible. In answer to a direct question from Washington, the headquarters of Eighth Air Force replied that to neutralize these five bases completely 250 sorties against each base per week for eight weeks would be required.
—from *The Army Air Forces in World War II*
by Wesley F. Craven
and James L. Cate

left: A crewman from *U-175* is saved as he grabs a boarding net of the cutter *Duane*.

When the Lord created man, he gave him two ends, one to sit on, and one to think with. Ever since that day man's success or failure has been dependent on the one he uses the most. It has been always, and is now, a case of heads you win and tails you lose.
—from *Tee Emm,* RAF publication

Child of delight! with sunbright hair, / And seablue eyes; / Spirit of Bliss, what brings thee here, / Beneath these sullen skies?
—from *The Two Children* by Emily Bronte

left: A submariner from *U-175* calls out for help from the *Spencer* shortly after the cutter had sunk his boat. Calm, relatively warm waters eased the rescue of the German crewmen.

LOSING IT

At the end of the war, all German naval vessels and submarines still afloat were divided among the four so-called great powers. England, Russia, the United States, and France, each got a dozen or so U-boats under an agreement whereby all these craft would be sunk in deep water or scrapped within two years. As the two year limit approached, we got ready to carry out our agreement and word reached me that the *U-505* was to be taken out with the surrendered U-boats and sunk. I immediately objected on the ground that the *U-505* was not included in the Four Power Agreement, which applied only to U-boats surrendered at the end of the war. The *U-505* had not surrendered, she was captured in battle on the high seas. She was therefore, U.S. property with no strings attached and we could keep

UNTIL AUGUST 1945, when two atom bombs convinced the Japanese that their only option was surrender, it had always been accepted that wars were never won until the enemy's army was defeated in the field. In Europe, three months earlier, as the soldiers of the Western Allies and the Soviet Union had converged upon Berlin, it had seemed that the axiom held good. Some questions, however, still remained. For example, there were grounds for asking whether the same result could not have been attained, and at a lesser cost, if the Allied bombers had concentrated all their mighty efforts of 1943 and 1944 on depriving Germany of oil. On the other hand, it could be argued that there might have been a different outcome if, in 1940 or 1941, Admiral Dönitz had been able to deploy the three hundred ocean raiders he had wanted and been given active air support; or indeed if Hitler, frustrated by the stalemate in the west, had not turned on Russia in 1942. However that might be, the Allies' victory saved the world from the nightmare of Nazi domination.

Of all the factors that contributed to that victory, moral and physical, military and technical, strategic and tactical, none was more important than the long campaign that kept the oceans open to traffic, without which Britain could not have survived, let alone provide the springboard for the Normandy invasion. In assessing that campaign, pride of place must go to the courage and endurance of the merchant seamen (and the fact that many were of foreign stock yet chose to risk their lives for the cause of the Western Allies, was something the U-boat men could never understand). Next in importance came the massive aid to Britain from North America in the shape of the "Cash and Carry" programme, the "Lend-Lease" package of destroyers, a squadron of Liberators and two of Flying Fortresses, the Canadian and American share in convoy duties, and the activities of the Tenth Fleet—aid reciprocated westward by Britain's

her as long as we wanted. I had no immediate plans in mind for the sub at this time, but my boys had gone to a lot of trouble to prevent that U-boat from sinking off the coast of Africa, and I took a dim view of scuttling her now. Government bureaucrats always like to have some precedent or a piece of paper to justify what they are doing and there were no precedents for this case. But I raised such a fuss that the Navy Department finally changed its mind rather dubiously and vetoed the scuttling order.
—from *Twenty Million Tons Under The Sea* by Rear Admiral Daniel V. Gallery, USN

The Englishman, be it noted, seldom resorts to violence; when he is sufficiently goaded he simply opens up, like the oyster, and devours his adversary.
—from *The Wisdom of the Heart* by Henry Miller

overleaf: *The Campbell Meets Her Enemy*, by Anton Otto Fischer.

years of experience in escort tactics, a fleet of armed trawlers, "huff-duff" (HFDF) radio and Ultra intelligence.

The third factor was the arrival, just in time, of very long-range aircraft, equipped with high-tech radar, to close the mid-Atlantic gap. There was no doubting the effectiveness of radar, especially in poor visibility or when there was low cloud, but more U-boats were detected by "huff-duff" and the good old human eye than by "the seeing radio" (as Henry L. Stimson, the US Secretary for War, rightly called it). Dönitz and his staff, however, constantly over-estimated its importance and, ill-advised by their scientists, took precautions against it that were ineffective. It was the combination of the centimetric radar and the massive growth of air power that eventually made the surface of the seas a U-boat killing ground.

The fourth contribution was made by Commander (later Captain) Frederick John Walker. By 1943 the offensive team tactics he had evolved to beat the German wolfpacks had been adopted by the Royal Navy and by the US Navy's hunter-killer groups. Walker's *Black Swan*-class sloops behaved on the ocean like a bucket in a maelstrom (even the hardiest sailor could feel queasy in a sloop), but they were highly manoeuvrable and, when in action, much like hounds on a scent; appropriately enough, it was Walker's practice to have "A-hunting We Will Go" played fortissimo on the ship's Tannoy when he sailed out of Liverpool in HMS *Starling*. His No. 2 Support Group sank twenty-one U-boats, including six in the course of one operation, and he himself destroyed *U-264*, the first snorkel boat to put to sea.

Along with Captain Donald Macintyre, "Johnny" Walker was recognized as the undoubted champion of anti-submarine warfare, and his efforts were acknowledged by the very rare award of the Distinguished Service Order with three bars—each the equal of another DSO. Worn out by his efforts, Walker died shortly after D-Day at the

age of forty-eight and was laid to rest at sea.

The last factor was the extremely valuable intelligence provided about U-boat movements by the cryptographers of the Government Code and Cypher School at Bletchley Park. It is probably true to say that the GC & CS played as significant a role in winning World War II as any other single unit, service or civilian.

The Signals Intelligence branch of GC & CS collected, collated and disseminated operational information obtained by eavesdropping on enemy communications. "Ultra" became the code-name for intelligence resulting from the interpretation of high grade codes and cyphers. The "Sigint" people's problem was that all security-graded radio traffic within Germany's armed forces was protected by the use of a highly sophisticated enciphering machine known as *Schlüssel-M* or "Enigma". In the use of Enigma, messages were typed on an ordinary keyboard and passed through electrical circuits to three rotors, which had separate contact points for every letter of the alphabet in a scrambled order. Each letter of the message, as the operator typed it, was transmitted in turn to the first, second and third rotors, changing each time, until the enciphered letter to be used by the operator was displayed on a screen above the keyboard and then transmitted in Morse code.

At the receiving end, an operator with a similar device and a list of rotor settings for the day, simply went through the enciphering routine in reverse. As the rotors could be changed at will, and the number of electrical circuits could be increased, the variations possible verged on the infinite. The machine was compact and simple to operate, and the resulting code was virtually impenetrable.

Bletchley Park House, a grand if unlovely mansion in rural Buckinghamshire, had been borrowed "for the duration" by His Majesty's Government from the business tycoon at whose whim it had been built. The accommodation was augmented by a cluster of utilitarian and yet more unlovely Nissen

The English may not like music, but they absolutely love the noise it makes.
—Sir Thomas Beecham

An Irishman fights before he reasons, a Scotchman reasons before he fights, an Englishman is not particular as to the order of precedence, but will do either to accommodate his customers.
—from *Lacon* by Charles Caleb Colton

left: A dock worker shows US soldiers the damage done by the attacks of RAF heavy bombers on this U-boat pen at Brest.

huts within the grounds, and it was there that the code-crackers—the academicians, senior wranglers, chess experts and crossword puzzlers—set about the task of unscrambling Enigma. Hour after hour, they listened to the mass of radio traffic but were not surprisingly unable to distinguish any sort of pattern: not only did each branch of the German forces have its own rotor settings, but the Naval code, known as Hydra, was altered every day; furthermore, the computing machines then available, although nearly as large as a deep freeze in a butcher's shop, were less powerful than a 1990s laptop computer. The first clue came from Poland, where an early version of Enigma had been made and whose intelligence service had monitored its development. By no means the least of Poland's contributions to the defeat of Germany was the story of Enigma that her agents sent to London. This was a beginning, but GC & CS still desperately needed information about the rotors and the codes. The Royal Navy was tasked with capturing a ship with the vital bits of gadgetry on board, and it did not fail.

In February 1940, *U-33* was captured while mine-laying in the Firth of Clyde, and three Enigma rotors came to hand; a month later cipher papers and another rotor were found on the armed trawler *Krebs*, and on 7th May 1941 the code settings for the next three months were discovered on the weather ship *München*. In each case it was announced for German ears that the vessels had gone down before they could be boarded.

Gradually the pieces were put together, and the big breakthrough came on the 9th May 1941, when a new Type IX boat, *U-110*, with Fritz-Julius Lemp in command, attacked a convoy off the coast of Greenland and hit two merchantmen with a fan of three torpedoes. Lemp, who had been severely reprimanded for sinking the British liner *Athenia* with 138 civilians aboard on the first day of the war, now made another mistake, and it was his last: lingering for a moment just below the surface to observe the results of his attack, his periscope was sighted from the crow's nest of an escorting

Number One, this is quite a moment. We have never seen the enemy before. They don't look very different from us, do they?
—from *The Cruel Sea* by Nicholas Montserrat

To die is poignantly bitter, but the idea of having to die without having lived is unbearable.
—from *Man for Himself* by Erich Fromm

Every tiny part of us cries out against the idea of dying, and hopes to live forever.
—Ugo Betti

left: A rescue party from the US Coast Guard cutter *Campbell* picking up survivors from their U-boat in 1943, in this painting by Anton Otto Fischer.

naval warship.

The corvette *Aubretia* attacked at once with depth charges, and *U-110* was forced to the surface, where she came under gunfire from *Aubretia* and two sister warships. Lemp and many of his crew had to abandon ship. The destroyer *Bulldog* was steaming in to ram when her captain, remembering the orders, saw a golden opportunity—this was a U-boat that could be captured in one piece. An armed boarding party found the code books and the Enigma machine intact. What happened to Lemp has never been clear—he either drowned himself or was shot while trying to scramble back on board. When King George VI pinned the Distinguished Service Cross on the chest of the commander of *Bulldog*'s boarding party, he had been well-briefed: he described the capture as "the most important event of the war at sea".

Once the machinery and documents had been examined at Bletchley Park, GC & CS knew many of Enigma's secrets and could read the naval Hydra code. It was essential, however, that Germany did not know this. Every man who had witnessed the capture of *U-110* was sworn to silence, and the secret was kept for another thirty years.

For the next nine months, Ultra intelligence served the British well: the position of every U-boat was plotted in the Admiralty's Submarine Tracking Room, and the shipping losses fell. Then, on 1st February 1942, the Hydra code was changed—not because Dönitz suspected it was broken but as a matter of routine—and the sinkings doubled in the three months that followed, until Ultra (which, by now, was being shared with the Americans) came back on stream. Another grim hiatus came in the spring of 1943, when a fourth rotor was added to Enigma. In the fortnight it took the crypto-analysts at Bletchley to find the answer, the wolfpacks ranged at will, and two unlucky convoys—the slow SC122 of fifty-four ships and the faster HX229 of forty, sailing from New York—suffered twenty-two losses. That slaughter, however, was the last of the Ubootwaffe's triumphs; May 1943 was to be known in Germany as "the month of the lost U-boats". From that time on, Ultra never failed. No wonder Winston Churchill called it "the precious secret".

The U-boats were still a threat, though, to which the Allies were devoting a hundred thousand men, over forty aircraft carriers and hundreds of destroyers, sloops and corvettes. But neither the advent of the snorkel, nor all the new gadgetry provided by German industry for the later types of U-boat towards the end of 1944 and in early 1945, could hide the writing on the wall: Germany had lost the battle for the sea lanes of the world. Although twenty-four Allied merchantmen were sunk between September and December 1944, it was at a cost of fifty-five U-boats. Brave though they were, and loyal to their Fatherland, most U-boat captains knew they were beaten, and so did their crews. Some still persisted in pressing home attacks against overwhelming odds, but others—more judicious—were content with softer targets, and as the war drew to an end the bitter knowledge of defeat was mixed with certain feelings of relief. Although all of the hardships and perils they had suffered had been in vain and although their Führer's dream of a thousand-year Reich was now never to be, at least they would not end their lives, like so many of their comrades, struggling hopelessly for breath on the bottom of the sea.

It had been a long, grim battle, fought on both sides with bravery, steadfastness and—generally, at least, a degree of honour. There were exceptions, however, such as an instance of a sinking U-boat's crew being fired on in the water by a British submarine and another, in 1944, of a U-boat's guns being turned on the lifeboats of a torpedoed Greek freighter. For the two commanders who were responsible for these actions, the outcome exemplified the difference between being on the winning and losing sides in war: the Royal Navy officer received a decoration—

...tonight our orders are, 'Bomb the centre of Bremen; make it uninhabitable for the workers.' England! Cricket! Huh! Justifiable? I do not know. I only know that I shall kill women and children soon.
—from *Journeys Into Night* by Don Charlwood

Operationally, the idea of area bombing was to attack an aiming point which lay at the centre of a large area whose destruction would be useful. It was, in other words, a method of making bombs which missed the aiming point contribute to the destruction of the German war machine. Since nearly all bombs were missing the aiming point, there was a certain logic about the idea.
—from *The Bombing Offensive Against Germany* by Noble Frankland

left: The ruins of Bremen at the end of the Allied bombing campaign which targeted key industrial sites such as the huge U-boat assembly yards.

albeit for another and more worthy feat—while the
U-boat commander, Kapitänleutnant Heinz Eck,
with four of his crew, was tried by court-martial,
found guilty of a war crime and shot by a British
firing squad on 30th November 1945.

While the Royal Navy killings passed quietly into
history, the U-boat incident became a *cause célèbre*.
There was a suspicion that the British only used it
to convince the Nuremberg Tribunal that Dönitz
had condoned such brutalities, and was thus guilty
of a war crime. If this was true, the ploy did not
succeed: Dönitz, while deprecating the action,
offered a reasonable excuse—his commanders were
expected to eliminate not the seamen but the
wreckage on the water, so that no trace would be
left that might assist the escort to hunt the U-boat
down. The Tribunal weighed the evidence and, in
so far as a war crime was concerned, found for the
Admiral.

The fact that the wretched Eck acted as he did
must be weighed against other occasions when
U-boat commanders, having come alongside a
lifeboat to discover the name and tonnage of the
vessel they had sunk, then provided the survivors
with sustenance, cigarettes, liquid (sometimes
Cognac) and a course to steer for land. In
November 1940 the survivors of the torpedoed
Laurentic, an Armed Merchant Cruiser (or
"Admiralty-made Coffin" in the sailor's phrase),
provided an instance of how such approaches
could be misconstrued. As described by Martin
Middlebrook in his fine book *Convoy*, the U-boat
surfaced, and the men in the lifeboats heard a
voice through the darkness, asking if they needed
food. Wary of a trap, the seamen did not answer.
Moments later, they heard the voice again.
"Goodnight, British", Otto Kretschmer called, and
U-99 stole silently away.

It was true that Dönitz's orders to his commanders
were that only downed airmen (who might give
useful information) were to be rescued from the sea,
and, considering the crowded conditions in a U-boat,

this was reasonable enough, but there was never any
proof that he approved the slaughter of survivors. For
their part, few U-boat commanders would attack
an escort ship while it was engaged in picking up
seamen from a stricken ship, but this was not entirely
for altruistic reasons—an escort so employed was
one less available for offensive action.

At least one other U-boat commander forgot, or
set aside, the rule about survivors. During the
night of 16th March 1942, a lone merchant
vessel, the 5,000-ton SS *Allendi*, was off the Ivory
Coast of West Africa and making for Freetown,
to join a convoy bound for England when the crew
heard what they thought was the sound of diesel
engines. They suspected that a surfaced U-boat
was charging its batteries nearby, and they were
right. Next morning *Allendi* was hit by a torpedo,
and began to sink. The Chief Radio Officer, Frank
Lewis, described what happened next:"The skipper
came into the radio cabin and said it was time for
us to get into the one remaining boat. We lost no
time, for the ship was riding very low in the water
by then. A good thing we did, too, because we had
not pulled very far away when another torpedo
struck her and she disappeared in just a few
minutes. There we were, thirteen in a small jolly-
boat that was damaged and water-logged."

It was at this point that the U-boat commander
made his offer. Coming alongside, he called down to
the survivors and gave them the choice of staying
where they were or being taken back to Germany as
prisoners of war. The men, most of whom were
Merchant Navy officers, chose to take their chances
in the jolly-boat. "When the U-boat left us", Lewis
continued, "she created such a wash that our boat
overturned, and we were left swimming. We had just
managed to clamber on to the upturned boat when
the next wash came along, righted the boat and threw
us back into the water." Nevertheless, the outcome
showed that the Merchant Navy men had made the
right decision: thirty-six hours later they pulled
ashore on the Ivory Coast and, eventually, made

194

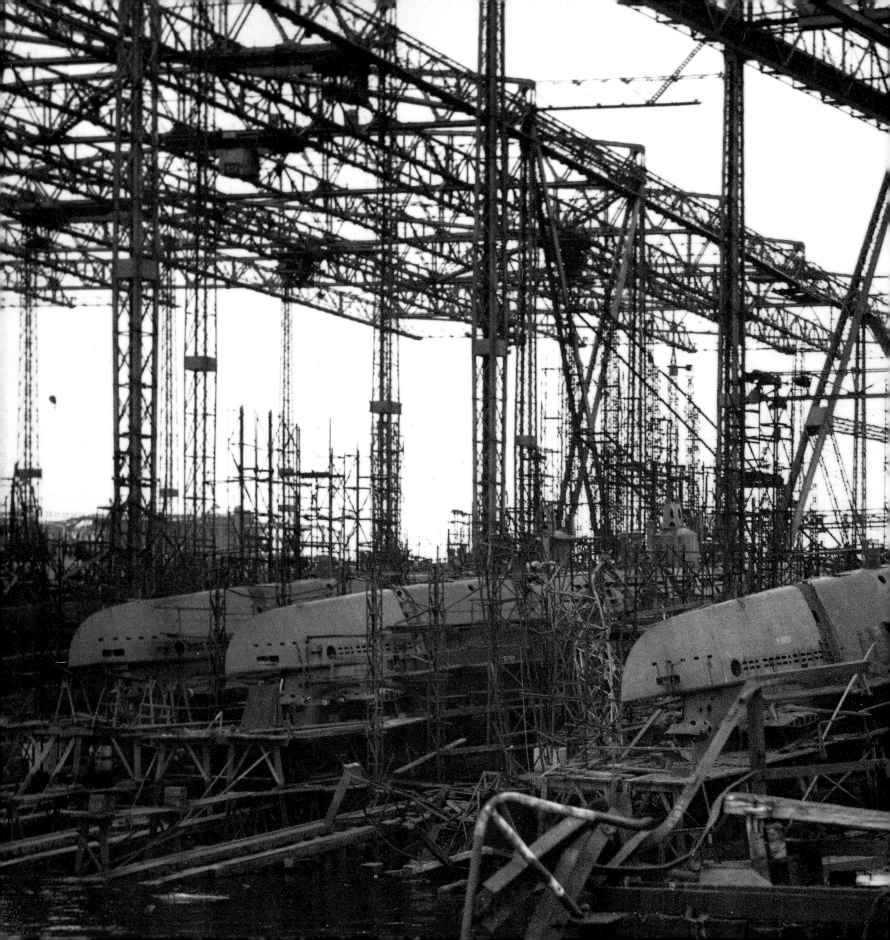

Gather ye rosebuds while ye may, / Old time is still a-flying, / And that same flower that smiles today / Tomorrow will be dying. / The glorious lamp of heaven, the sun, / The higher he's a-getting, / The sooner will his race be run, / And nearer he's to setting. / That age is best which is the first, / When youth and blood are warmer, / But being spent, the worse, and worst / Times still succeed the former.
—by Robert Herrick

left: The great U-bunker at Bordeaux in 1996.

Boys are the cash of war. Whoever said / We're not free-spenders doesn't know our likes.
—John Ciardi

right: Wallowing helplessly in the North Atlantic in August 1943, *U-185* has become the victim of a Fido acoustic torpedo dropped by an Allied aircraft. As the war progressed, Allied technology outpaced that of the Germans.

their long way home.

In the first week of June 1944, every German with the slightest notion of what was going on around him knew that the Allies were about to launch a great invasion, and that it would fall somewhere on the coast of France. Some believed that the Wehrmacht would wipe out the invaders before they got off the beaches; others that even if a few contrived to get ashore, the famed Atlantic Wall could not be breached. There were doubts, however, within the German High Command as to where the blow might fall. Feldmarschall von Rundstedt, the Army Commander in the West, held that the Allies would go for the shortest sea crossing, which meant the Pas de Calais area, while his colleague Feldmarschall Rommel, and indeed his Führer, were equally convinced about the coast of Normandy. Wherever it might be, it was sure to come and had to be withstood. In Erwin Rommel's view, lose the battle for the beaches, lose the war.

Nominally, von Rundstedt commanded fifty-eight divisions in the west, spread along the thousand miles of coastline and hinterland between the hook of Holland and the Spanish border, but so weakened was the German Army by the carnage on the Russian front that the real strength was less than half that number. The Luftwaffe, mauled for many months by the USAAF's mass formations and by the Allied fighters, was desperately short of pilots and of gasoline. As for the Kriegsmarine, Dönitz had known since the *Tirpitz* went down in November 1944 that the few remaining surface ships had no further role in World War II. He was obliged to turn to his ever-faithful Ubootwaffe—indeed, there was nowhere else to turn. According to his memoirs, his orders included the following words: "Every vessel taking part in the landing is a target of the utmost importance which must be attacked regardless of risk. Every boat that inflicts losses on the enemy while he is landing has fulfilled its function even

right: The Naval Enigma machine.

Nothing remains static in war or in military weapons, and it is consequently often dangerous to rely on courses suggested by apparent similarities in the past.
—Fleet Admiral Ernest J. King

Our opposite number in the British Admiralty, a branch of the Division of Naval Intelligence called 17-Zed, was participating in a phenomenally successful propaganda coup called the *Atlantik Sender* (Radio Atlantic). It was a full-scale radio transmission going on the whole day that pretended to be somewhere inside Germany, operated by some patriotic but anti-Nazi Germans, although it was actually operated at Woburn Abbey, the palatial seat of the Duke of Bedford, which Britain's Political Warfare Executive had taken over for the duration.
—from *The Tenth Fleet* by Ladislas Farrago

centre left: Enigma, the German enciphering and deciphering machine. above left: Bletchley Park where the British broke the Enigma codes. left: The radio room of *U-124* with the Enigma machine in the foreground. above centre: Woburn Abbey, the home of the British *Radio Atlantic* or *Atlantik Sender*.

Heinrich Heinck   Herbert Haupt   Werner Thiel   Herman Neubauer

Richard Quirin   Ernest Burger   George Dasch   Edward Kerling

above: Eight German saboteurs who were dispatched by U-boat to the east coast of the USA, to destroy targets such as the Alcoa aluminum plants. All eight were captured before they could carry out their assignments; six were sent to the electric chair, the other two were imprisoned.

BLUEBIRD

For best results use
RCA Victor Needles

B-11586-A

DER FUEHRER'S FACE--Bright Two-Step
(From the Walt Disney film "Der Fuehrer's Face")
(Oliver Wallace)
Spike Jones and his City Slickers

Life is full of chances and changes, and the most prosperous of men may in the evening of his days meet with great misfortunes.
—from *Nicomachean Ethics* by Aristotle

left: Captain Daniel V. Gallery, a US Navy 'hunter-killer' task group commander, decided to try to capture a U-boat, the *U-505,* when the opportunity arose on 4th June 1944. His task group attacked, boarded and captured the submarine, and began the trip back to the USA with *U-505* in tow. It marked the first time in American history since 1815 that a foreign enemy man-of-war had been boarded and captured on the high seas. Today, owing in large part to the additional efforts of Gallery, the *U-505* is on display at the Chicago Museum of Science and Industry.

though he perishes in so doing." It was a mark of how low the Nazi star had fallen since the days of the *Blitzkrieg* and "the happy time" that the U-boat, once one of Germany's prime weapons of attack, was to be committed, like the Luftwaffe before it, to defence.

Thirty-six of the surviving boats were in Bay of Biscay bunkers, with another twenty-two lying in Norwegian fiords. Fifteen of the 1st Flotilla were berthed in Brest and, on a fine May morning, when the trees were in leaf and the early flowers were showing their colours, the commanders were told what their Admiral would require of them when "Overlord" was launched. As Herbert Werner, who was one of those commanders, describes in his *Iron Coffins*, the order was to "attack and sink the invasion fleet with the final objective of destroying enemy ships by ramming". If Werner's recollection is correct (and Erich Topp supports it, although there are some who dispute it), the words provided one final, dark analogy with the combat fliers—not, however, with the Allied bomber crews but with the Kamikaze pilots of Japan.

The commanders waited grimly for their sailing orders, and eventually they came at midnight on 6th June. Werner's *U-415* was one of eight U-boats, none of them equipped with a snorkel, which left the harbour, escorted by trawlers and patrol boats, through the inlet and out into the bay. As Werner relates it, the orders were to proceed at top speed on the surface to the south coast of England, and there to carry out the duties for which they had been briefed—suicidally, if need be. Two days later *U-415* limped back into Brest, badly damaged—one of only three boats to survive the mission. Meanwhile, seven snorkel-fitted boats had sailed for the Baie de la Seine, but the impact they could make on the vast armada of 4,000 landing craft and 800 warships was insignificant. "By 30th June", Werner wrote, "U-boat operations since the invasion began were a full-fledged disaster. We had sunk five Allied cargo ships and two destroyers, and we had lost twenty-two U-boats."

Death has but one terror, that it has no tomorrow.
—from *The Passionate State of Mind*
by Eric Hoffer

One thing is sure, there are just two respectable ways to die. One is of old age, and the other is by accident.
—from *The Philistine*
by Elbert Hubbard

Our last garment is made without pockets.
—Italian proverb

left: As the carrier *Guadalcanal* (not shown in photograph) takes up slack in the towline, the *U-505* rises slowly and the long journey into captivity begins. overleaf: U-boats tied up at Wilhelmshaven.

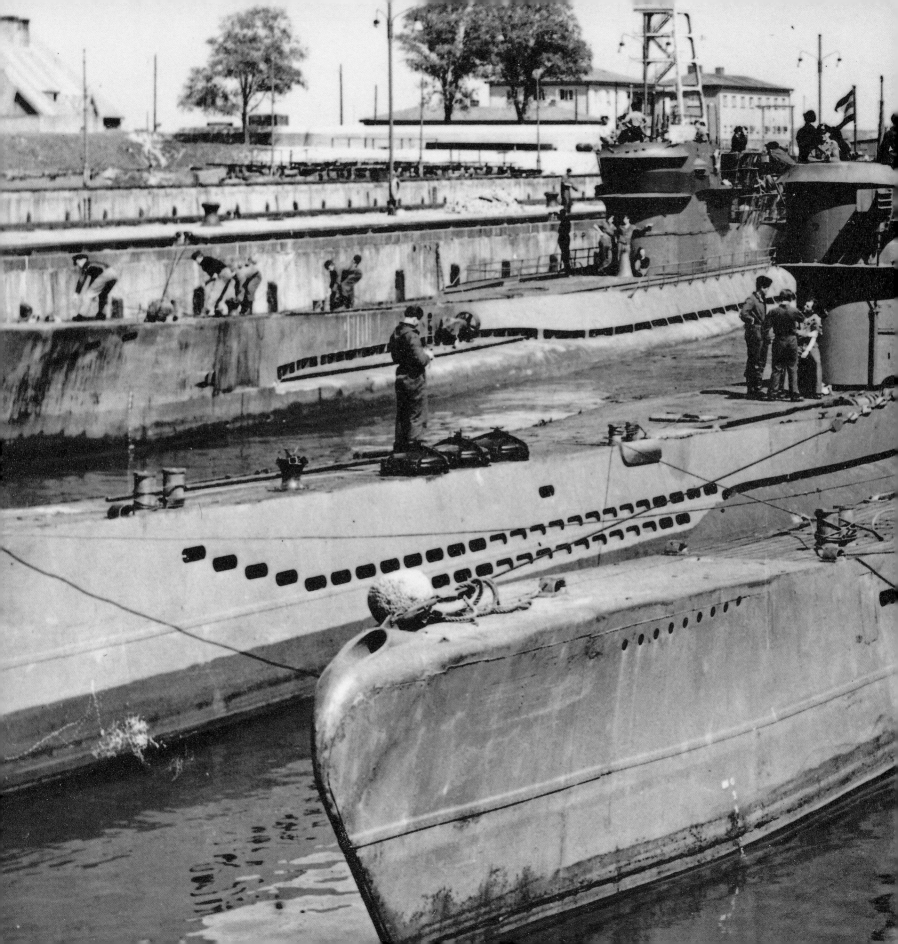

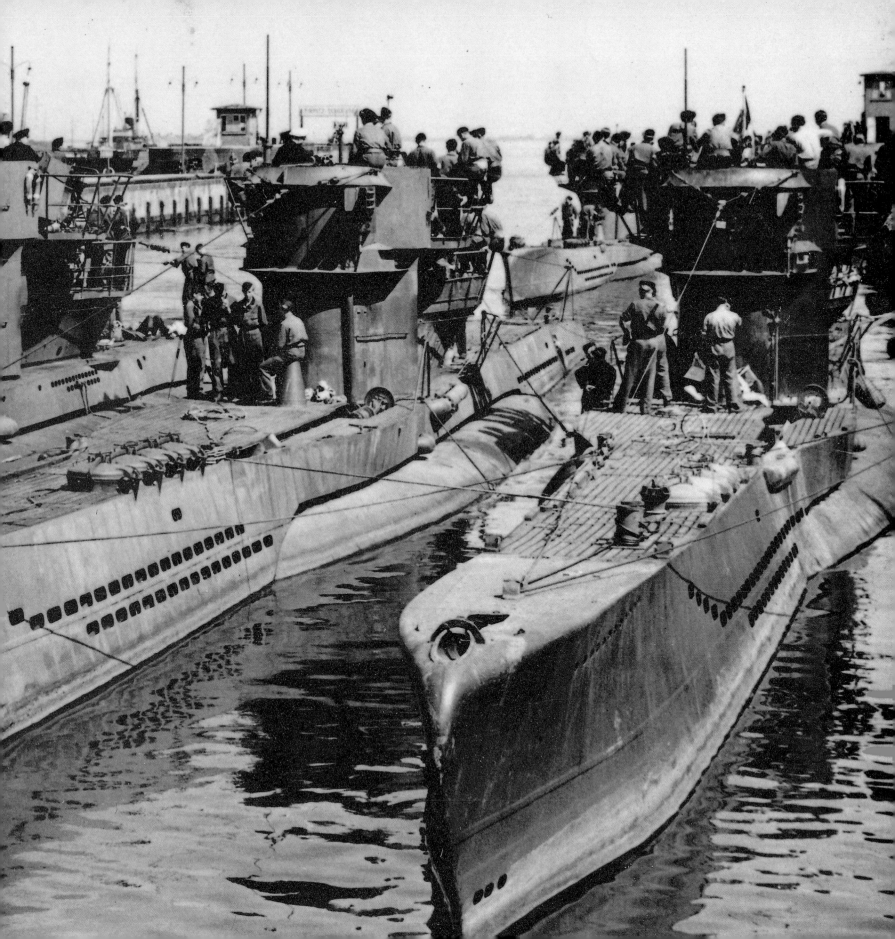

American tanks rolled in to Brittany, and the RAF pounded Saint-Nazaire, Lorient and Brest. By September Brest was under siege, encircled by the US 6th Armoured Division, and the Bay of Biscay bases were no longer tenable. The remaining U-boats were sent on a hazardous six-week voyage around the coast of Ireland, through the North Channel, past the Orkney Islands and the Shetlands, harassed by aircraft and warships all the way, to anchor in Bergenfiord on the southwest coast of Norway. The contrast between Bergen's gaunt, glacial landscape, grey seas and chilling fogs, and the memory of the sunshine, pleasant promenades and cafés that had been left behind, underlined the decline in the fortunes of the U-boat arm. Although there were to be a number of determined offensive patrols in British coastal waters in the ensuing months, and one last desperate mission to the east coast of America in the spring of 1945, the retreat from France was to mark the end of

above left: *U-3008*, a Type XXI boat seen in US Navy hands at New London, Conn. in late August 1945. below: A Snorkel-equipped boat, the *U-234*, was surrendered and brought into Portsmouth, NH, on 19th May 1945. below left: The *U-505* as she was finally positioned at the Chicago Museum of Science and Industry.

The float of the Schnorkel had jammed in closed position, and with the air intake cut off, the port engine had sucked most of the air out of the hull before the diesel could be halted. The Chief's orders died in the thinned air. The men gasped for air, their eyes bulging. The Chief lowered the boat, bringing the Schnorkel head below surface in an effort to loosen the float. To no avail. Breathing became ever more difficult; suffocation seemed imminent. The Chief gesticulated wildly, trying to tell his men to lay down the air mast, which might result in unlocking the float. With agonizing effort, the mechanics turned handles, lowered the mast by cable, then erected it again with the primitive winch. Painful minutes passed, but then the mast drained and the seawater gargled down the bilges. The float cleared with a snap and air was sucked

into the boat with a long sigh. The sudden change in pressure burst many an eardrum. Some of the men covered their faces in pain and sagged to the deck plates. Others swallowed violently to equalize the pressure.
—from *Iron Coffins*
by Herbert A. Werner

And this I hate—not men, nor flag nor race, / But only war with its wild, grinning face.
—from *The Hymn of Hate*
by Joseph Dana Miller

When after many battles past, / Both tir'd with blows, make peace at last, / What is it, after all, the people get? / Why! taxes, widows, wooden legs, and debt.
—from *Almanack*
by Francis Moore

the Ubootwaffe's effective part in World War II.

Berlin's communiqués continued to be highly optimistic. In September the German people were informed that a new and devastating weapon, the V-2 rocket, which even then was falling on England and would soon fall on America, was sure to make the Allies sue for peace; in December the news was that the Army's great offensive in the hills of the Ardennes was about to hurl the British and Americans back into the sea; in February 1945 it was announced that the Führer had taken personal command of the capital's defences; in April, that the death of the American president, always Britain's friend, would result in a breach between the western Allies. The facts, however, were that the British withstood the flying bombs and rockets in the same sturdy way they had endured the Blitz, that the Ardennes offensive was halted and crushed within ten days, that Franklin D. Roosevelt was succeeded in the White House by a man no less dedicated to the defeat of Germany than he, and that the only command Hitler could exercise from his bunker in Berlin was over the immediate circle of his entourage. Just before midnight on 1st May the sombre strains of Wagner, seldom known to introduce good news, preceded a special broadcast bulletin, which included one last piece of Nazi fiction: "Our Führer, fighting to his last breath, fell for Germany in his Headquarters..."

At the end of World War I Germany's U-boats had been surrendered in droves, while seventy of the Kaiser's captured surface ships, in a last defiant act, had been scuttled by their crews in Scapa Flow; in 1945 Germany's sailors believed that the Nazi fleet, including the U-boat arm, should follow that example. The signal to commanders was to be the code-word *Regenbogen* "Rainbow", but the Grand Admiral never sent the signal. The British had stipulated that there must be no demolition and no scuttling of vessels, otherwise the bombing of strategic targets—or what remained of them—would

go on. Dönitz had no choice: on 5th May 1945 he sent the order to his U-boats to transmit their positions in plain language and sail to Allied ports. "Unbeaten and unblemished", he added to the message, "you lay down your arms after a heroic fight without parallel."

Germany, at that point, still had a strength of over 350 U-boats, including many new Type XXIs and XXIIIs, which had never been in action. Of these, the majority were moored in German ports or at anchor in the fiords. Of those remaining at sea, two were sailed to Argentina by their hard case commanders, while the rest headed for Britain or America, in accordance with their orders, hoisting the black flag of piracy, which, for the occasion, was to signify surrender. Many boats, however, were commanded by men who either could not believe, or could not accept, their Admiral's last order. They exchanged signals on the old combat frequency, and the word that passed between them was *Regenbogen*. In the waters of the Baltic and in the North Sea over two hundred U-boats were scuttled by their crews.

By September 1945, 156 U-boats had been surrendered, and of those that fell into the Royal Navy's hands, 110 were either scuttled or sunk by gunfire in 300 feet of water off the coast of Northern Ireland, where they remain.

In 1943, dining with Winston Churchill, Air Chief Marshal Harris had promised that, if the United States Eighth Air Force would join with his Command in the Battle of Berlin, it might "cost five hundred aircraft but it would cost Germany the war". That same year Grossadmiral Dönitz had been trying to tell his Führer, in more guarded terms, that given more and better vessels, adequate intelligence and air reconnaissance, his U-boat arm could bring the Allies down. The likelihood is that Churchill nodded and poured another brandy, and that Hitler changed the subject to the Russian front. No one will ever know whether the Air Chief Marshal or the Admiral was right; what is sure is that neither got his way.

Death is the supple suitor /
That wins at last— /
It is a stealthy wooing /
Conducted first / By pallid
innuendoes / And dim
approach / But brave at last
with Bugles.
—Emily Dickinson

left: A U-boat crewman
is rescued after the
sinking of his boat by the
Canadian frigate
Swansea in late 1944.

below left: Prisoners from the crew of *U-175* are marched ashore by British Marines at Gourock, Scotland. In the background are the vessels involved in their sinking and rescue, the *Spencer* and the *Duane*.
below: U-boat men from the crew of *U-858*, having become prisoners of war.

Many strokes, though with
a little axe, hew down and
fell the hardest-timber'd
oak.
—from *Henry VI
Pt. III*, Act II, Sc 1
by Shakespeare

left: Crewmen of the
U-291, commanded by
Hermann Neumeister,
as their boat is tied up
alongside a pier at
Wilhelmshaven.

U-BOAT

FIELD MARSHAL Montgomery accepted Germany's unconditional surrender to the Allied powers from General Jodl on 7th May 1945. That evening the Canadian steamer *Avondale Park*, with the barnacled Norwegian tramp *Sneland I*, which had lived through the horrors of convoy SC7 in October 1940 and many more wartime adventures, sailed past the lights of Edinburgh, through the Firth of Forth and into the North Sea. Shortly after 11 p.m. both ships were sinking—destroyed by

torpedoes from the lone patrolling *U-2336*. Whether Kapitänleutnant Emil Klusmeier failed to receive the cease-fire order or elected to ignore it has never been determined; what is certain is that he fired the last shots of the European war at sea.

On average, the U-boats sank a ship for every day of the sixty-eight months that the war in Europe lasted, and they accounted for 69 per cent of all the Allies' shipping losses. The tonnages claimed by their commanders were occasionally exaggerated;

far left: A stained-glass window detail from the German Naval Memorial at Laboé. centre: The U-boat memorial near Kiel. below: The *U-995*.

below: *U-94* arrives at Saint-Nazaire 31st May 1941. Kapitänleutnant Herbert Kuppisch is in command.

God and our sailors we adore, / When danger threatens, not before. / With danger past, both are requited. / God forgotten, the sailor slighted.
—Old saying

It is not the going out of port, but the coming in, that determines the success of a voyage.
—from *Proverbs from Plymouth Pulpit* by Henry Ward Beecher

for example, in November 1942 the Ubootwaffe claimed a million tons and the Allies admitted to 750,000 tons, although the real figure was 637,000. However, such discrepancies were not entirely surprising—the claims of successes by Allied fighter pilots and bomber crews were seldom conservative. It was quite possible, in the heat of battle and certainly in darkness, when more than one assailant had attacked the same target, that each might believe he had made the kill. The true figures were disastrous enough: a loss to the Allies of 2,603 merchant and 175 naval ships with a total displacement of 14,500,000 tons, and of the lives of 30,246 merchant seamen,

I am not now that which I have been.
—from *Childe Harold*
by George Gordon Lord Byron

far left: Relaxing on the "wintergarden" of *U-100* near Lorient in September 1940. centre left: Pleasure boats in one of the boxes of the Bordeaux pen, left: Defensive gun ports in the bomb-proof lock at Saint-Nazaire. below left: One of the torpedo bunkers at La Pallice, 1996.

A man has his distinctive personal scent which his wife, his children and his dog can recognize. A crowd has a generalized stink.
—W.H. Auden

223

including 5,000 Americans—one of every four who went to sea. It was a casualty rate similar to that of the Allied servicemen who became prisoners of the Japanese.

The Ubootwaffe's losses were even more severe. Although documented casualty figures tend to vary slightly, of 39,000 men who went to sea in U-boats during World War II, the U-boat memorial near Kiel records a death roll of 27,491, and it is known that a further 5,000 were made prisoners of war. Of the 863 U-boats that sailed on operational patrols, 754 were lost. These were losses even more

far left: A U-boat under air attack. below: A Blast-proof door at the Lorient Keroman III U-bunker.

How are the mighty fallen!
—II Samuel. I. 25

225

above: *U-373* crossing
the Bay of Biscay in April
1942 under command of
Oberleutnant zur See
Loeser. right and far right:
The *U-995* displayed at
Laboé near Kiel.

right: Forward torpedo room of *U-505* as it appeared when the boat was captured by the US Navy task group 22.3 in June 1944.

disastrous than those of World War I. Then, of the 800 U-boats built, 343 were in combat and 199 lost, taking the lives of 5,249 seamen. One more statistic is a strange one and, in its own way, almost as tragic for the U-boat arm: of the 1,162 World War II U-boats commissioned, leaving aside the refuellers and the training boats, 550 never sank a ship.

Since the first days of the war, when they slipped out of harbour with the song "Denn wir fahren gegen Engelland" on their lips and in their hearts, the men of the U-boat arm were romantically portrayed to the German people as "knights of the deep", sailing their "grey wolves" off to war, or as a "band of brothers" fighting in "steel sharks"; later, when the casualty rolls began to grow, they were to be thought of as a "crusade of children" sailing in their "iron coffins".

Putting propaganda and romanticism aside, the fact remains that the U-boat men fought a long and epic struggle against the ever more overwhelming weapons of the Allied forces—a struggle that, for at least the last year of the war, they must have known they could not win. In the later days, it must have seemed to them a question not of whether they would die but of where and when. In their "small, dim world below the sea" they showed great courage and tenacity, loyalty and fortitude—qualities worthy of a better cause. It was their misfortune and their tragedy that the cause for which they fought was vile and unacceptable to the great mass of humanity. Had the U-boats been successful in the Atlantic battle, and in the first six months of 1942 it looked as though they would be, the deaths of millions would have been sure to follow and the cruel subjugation of many millions more. Victory for them, for the Nazis and their allies, would have surely brought the dawning of a new dark age. While the prodigious efforts and steadfast conduct of the U-boat men can always be admired and recorded with respect in the long history of warfare, there must also be rejoicing that they failed.

228

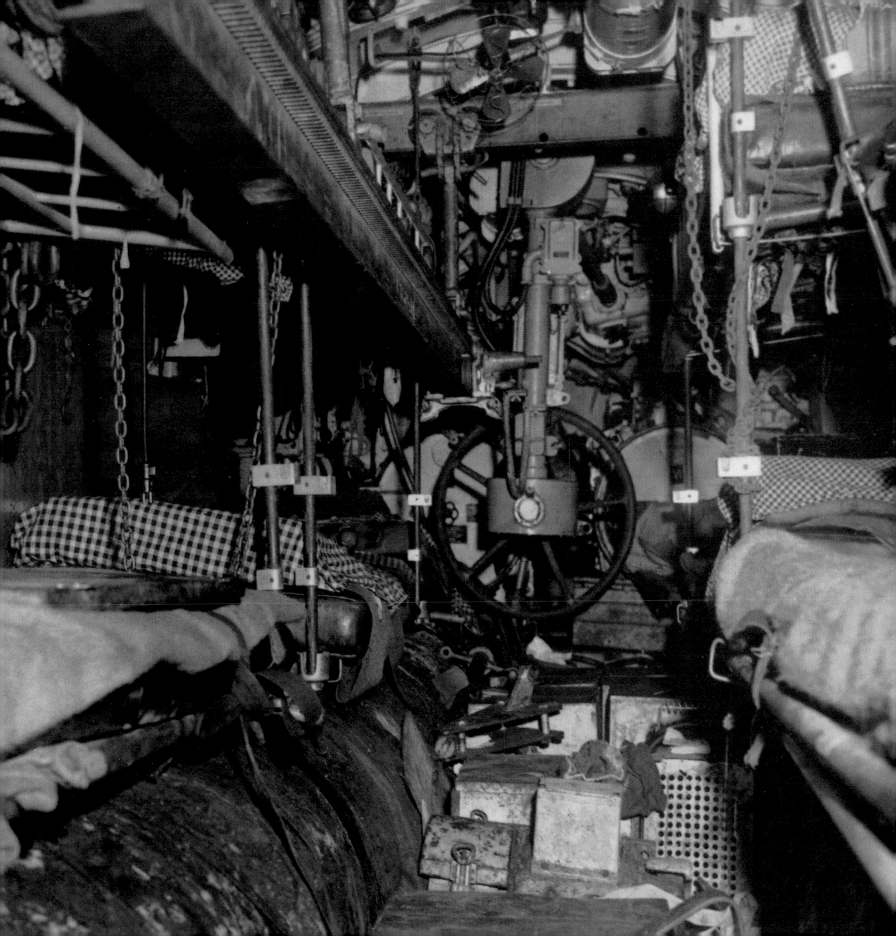

left: The baton of Gross-admiral Karl Dönitz. far left: The La Cambe cemetery near the beaches of Normandy, where many German casualties of the Allied invasion fighting are buried. Unlike their comrades at La Cambe, most of the 27,491 who sailed and perished in the U-boats have no grave and no marker.

On May 8, 1945, I was at the 2nd Army HQ on Luneburg Heath, a Captain on intelligence duties—but I took part in the events which marked the final collapse of the Nazi regime two weeks later. ...I was one of four British officers detailed to arrange the final arrest on May 23 of senior German government officials still at liberty in Flensburg on the Baltic coast. It was all very friendly when they surrendered. Among our charges were Gross Admiral Dönitz, General Jodl and Reichminister Albert Speer. I took Admiral Dönitz's baton on the excuse that he did not need it anymore. It's now in the regimental museum.
—Hugh Williams TD
Flitwick, Bedford

The night is dark , and I am far from home.
—from *Lead, Kindly Light* by John Henry Newman

GLOSSARY

AA Anti-aircraft.

AAF (US) Army Air Forces.

Abaft toward the stern of a boat or ship.

Abt Abteilung / department or division.

Adressbuch U-boat code book used in disguising ocean chart grid positions in radio transmissions.

AGRU Front Ausbildungsgruppe Front / a technical testing branch to evaluate submarines and crews before releasing them to operational duty.

Alarm! emergency dive order on a U-boat.

Angle-on-the-bow variance between line-of-sight on a U-boat, and the compass heading of its target.

Aphrodite German device used to confuse radar by reflecting impulses.

Armed Guard US Navy gun crew serving aboard a merchant ship.

ASDIC acronym for the British Anti-Submarine Detection Investigation Committee; the name given to a device housed in a dome under the hull of an anti-submarine vessel and used in detecting the presence of submerged submarines.

ASV airborne microwave radar (10 and 3 cm).

ASW anti-submarine warfare.

Athos radio detection antenna.

Bachstelze (water-stilt) autogiro-like device towed on a cable behind a U-boat to improve the field of vision of the 'flying' look-out.

Bali a radar detection aerial.

Bauwerft a ship-building yard.

B-Dienst Funkbeobachtungsdienst / German radio-monitoring and cryptographic intelligence service.

BdU Befehlshaber der Unterseeboote / Commander in Chief, U-boats (referred specifically to Admiral Karl Dönitz, but also in reference to his staff or headquarters.

Betasom The Italian submarine command based in Bordeaux.

Biscay, Bay Atlantic bay extending from northwestern France to northern Spain, the area in which the main German U-boat pen shelters were located.

Biscay Cross nickname of the early radar detection aerial used on U-boats.

Bletchley Park the British Government Code and Cipher School located in a large country house in Buckinghamshire, north of London.

Bold a device used by U-boats to confuse ASDIC.

Bombe a linked series of Enigma machines, devised at Bletchley Park.

Boot a German boat or warship; the commander is not a staff officer, and the second-in-command is called First Watch Officer, i.e. on a submarine.

Bootskanone gun on the foredeck of a U-boat.

Bow forward end of a vessel.

Bow caps small doors at the outside ends of a submarine's torpedo tubes.

Bows forward exterior hull of a vessel.

Bunkers exterior fuel tanks on a U-boat.

Calibre the measurement of gun and shell size, taken from the internal diameter, or bore, of the gun barrel, i.e. a 5-inch shell is not 5 inches long, but 5 inches in diameter.

Casing a submarine's outer skin of light plating, which encloses the ballast tanks and pressure hull.

Cipher a secret letter-substitution communication code system.

Conn steering responsibility for a boat or ship.

Conning tower the observation tower or platform of a submarine; on a U-boat it contained steering controls; on type IX U-boats it contained the attack periscope eyepiece and torpedo deflection calculator.

Contact pistol torpedo detonator that explodes on striking a solid object.

Control room Zentrale the U-boat diving control facility, located below the conning tower and bridge.

Convoy a precise assembly of merchant ships organized in columns and escorted by warships.

Corvette a highly manoeuvrable armed escort ship, smaller than a destroyer.

Cypern a type of radar detector.

DD US Navy reference to a destroyer-class warship.

DE a destroyer escort-class warship.

To be alive at all involves some risk.
—Harold Macmillan

Decrypt a deciphered or decoded message.

Destroyer Germans used this term for all small vessels employed in convoy protection and often included frigates and corvettes in this category.

Dienst Duty.

Dienstgrad Rank.

Dienstelle Headquarters.

D-maschine Diesel engine.

Displacement the weight of a boat or ship, as measured by the amount of water displaced when placing the boat or ship in water.

Dräger Tauchretter underwater escape apparatus for U-boat crewmen (made by the firm Dräger).

Eel (Aal) U-boat nickname for a torpedo.

EK Eisernes Kreuz. Iron Cross award.

E-maschinen electric motors.

Encryption enciphered or encoded message.

Englisch a common German reference term to everything Allied or British during WWII.

Enigma the Schlussel M cipher machine (also used in reference to the machine's encrypted product).

Fächerschuss simultaneous spread or fan-launch of two or more torpedoes.

Fähnrich zur See Midshipman.

Fangschuss *coup de grâce* or finishing shot.

FAT (Federapparat Torpedo) an anti-convoy weapon that travelled in a straight line for a predetermined distance and then zigzagged.

Fathom six feet or 1.829 metres.

FdU (Führer der Unterseeboote) Flag Officer for Submarines.

Feindfahrt operational patrol.

Flak (Fliegerabwehrkanone) anti-aircraft gun.

Fliege Fly. A radar detector.

Flotilla small fleet of small vessels.

Flugboot German for flying-boat aircraft.

Fregattenkapitän Captain (junior).

Freya a radar detection apparatus.

Frontboot U-boat at sea that has entered an operational area.

Funk-Telegraphie (FT) German reference for Wireless Telegraphy radio transmission/reception.

Funker German Navy radioman.

Funkmess radio/radar detection.

Funkpeilgerät radio direction finder.

Great Circle shortest route, following arc of the earth's surface.

Grossadmiral grand admiral, corresponding to Fleet Admiral (US).

GRT gross register tonnage, the total displacement of a ship.

Gruppe group.

HE (hydrophone effect) underwater sound such as propeller cavitation of a surface ship.

Hedgehog a type of anti-U-boat bomb thrown ahead of the vessel carrying it.

HF/DF (Huff-Duff) high-frequency/direction finder.

Hundekurve (dog curve) track taken by a U-boat in attacking a ship, to present the smallest possible profile to the enemy at all times.

Hydra cipher used by U-boats in establishing the daily setting of the Enigma/Schlussel M cipher machine.

Hydrophone underwater sound detection device.

Hydroplanes extended rudder surfaces on submarine hull that make the boat go up and down when it is underwater.

Jumping wire heavy cable with a cutting edge, stretched from bow to stern over the submarine's conning tower, to cut or deflect underwater obstacles such as nets.

Kaleu, Kaleunt diminutive forms of the naval rank Kapitänleutnant.

Kapitänleutnant Lieutenant Commander.

Kalipatrone Potash-cartridge respirator that absorbed carbon dioxide.

Keroman protective U-boat bunkers at Pointe de Keroman near the Lorient harbour entrance.

Kleine boot small training submarine, i.e. type IID.

KM (Kriegsmarine) the German Navy, 1935–1945.

Km Kilometre.

Knot a ship's speed measured as one nautical mile per hour.

Konteradmiral Rear Admiral.

Death is the next step after the pension—it's perpetual retirement without pay.
—from *The Enchanted* by Jean Giraudoux

Do not seek death. Death will find you. But seek the road which makes death a fulfillment.
—from *Markings* by Dag Hammarskjöld

Always design a thing by considering it in its next larger context—a chair in a room, a room in a house, a house in an environment, an environment in a city plan.
—Eliel Saarinen

Korvettenkapitän Commander.

Krieg war.

Kriegstagebuch (KTB) German war diary kept by boats and ships at sea and by shore-based headquarters staffs.

Kurzsignale a U-boat's short-signal radio position report.

Leutnant zur See Lieutenant junior grade.

LI (Leitender Ingenieur) Chief Engineering Officer.

Löwe Lion. Nickname for Karl Dönitz.

Luftwaffe German Air Force.

M.A.N. Maschinenfabrik Augsburg-Nürnberg AG, the manufacturer of diesel engines for the Type VII and IX U-boats.

Manoeuvering room electric motor room on U-boat.

Metox a type of German radar detector.

Milch cow nickname for a U-boat used for re-supply and re-fuelling of other U-boats.

Mixers torpedo mates on a U-boat.

Naxos a radar detection device.

ObdM (Oberbefehlshaber der Marine) Supreme C-in-C of the German Navy.

Oberfähnrich zur See Ensign.

Oberleutnant zur See Lieutenant senior grade.

Papenberg column a shallow depth-pressure gauge.

Paukenschlag to beat on the kettle drums—a code name for the initial U-boat attack on the United States.

Periscope extendable tubelike optical device containing prisms, mirrors and lenses that enable a U-boat crew member to view the sea surface while the boat is submerged.

Radar radio detection and ranging.

Rake a patrol line of several U-boats across the path of a convoy.

Reichsmarine the German Navy, 1919–1935.

Ritterkreuz the Knight's Cross decoration.

Rohr torpedo tube.

Rudeltaktik technique of massing U-boats in a 'wolfpack' patrol line across a convoy's course and engaging the ships of the convoy in a radio-coordinated attack.

Schlüssel M the Kriegsmarine version of the Enigma cipher machine.

Schnorchel/Schnorkel a valved air pipe that protruded above the surface and allowed a submerged U-boat to proceed on diesel power.

Schussmeldung a U-boat's 'shooting report', required after each action.

Sea cow nickname for large U-boats.

Sea force recorded in a U-boat's KTB on an ascending scale from zero to ten.

Soda-lime a chemical used to absorb moisture and carbon dioxide breathed into the air by the crew of a submarine during a prolonged dive.

Sonar acronym for Sound Navigation and Ranging (US).

Spargel literally, asparagus, U-boat nickname for the periscope.

Special Intelligence decrypted wireless German radio traffic, from Bletchley Park near London.

Squid an Allied anti-submarine mortar weapon.

Standzielsehrohr the attack periscope sight in a U-boat conning tower.

Tetis a U-boat cipher used in wireless transmissions by new U-boats in training.

Tiefenmesser a U-boat's depth-pressure gauge.

Torpex a high-explosive mix of Cyclonite, TNT and aluminum flakes.

Trim the balancing of a submarine's weight and equilibrium underwater.

U-boot underwater boat, German submarine.

Ubootwaffe the German submarine fleet.

Unterseeboot the German term for submarine.

Verloren lost, sunk.

Vernichtet destroyed.

Versenkt sunk.

Vorhaltrechner a Siemens-made electro-mechanical deflection calculator in the a U-boat conning tower that fed attack coordinates into the gyrocompass steering mechanism of the torpedoes in their tubes.

Wabos German nickname for Wasserbombe.

Wasserbombe German term for depth charge dropped on a U-boat by British and American surface ships and aircraft.

Wanze a radar detection device.

Wehrmacht the German Army.

Weyer a U-boat's identification manual for the warships of all nations.

Werft shipyard or dockyard.

Wind force wind velocities were recorded in a U-boat's KTB on an ascending scale from zero to ten.

Wintergarten German nickname for the open, railed platform on the after part of a U-boat bridge. The British referred to it as a 'bandstand'.

Wolfpack Rudel in German; an attack technique developed by Admiral Karl Dönitz.

Working up the time allotted for officers and crewmen to familiarize themselves with their new boat prior to sailing on their first patrol in her.

Zaunkönig the German acoustic torpedo, also known as T5.

Zentrale the U-boat control room, directly below the conning tower and bridge, containing all diving controls.

ZEICHNET
KRIEGS-ANLEIHE
FÜR U-BOOTE GEGEN
ENGLAND

235

below: An old neighbourhood in Brest, home port and the headquarters for 1 and 9 U-Flotille.

EQUIVALENT KRIEGSMARINE AND US NAVY RANKS

GERMAN OFFIZIERE MIT PATENT / US NAVY COMMISSIONED OFFICERS
Grossadmiral / Commander in Chief, Fleet Admiral
Generaladmiral / Admiral, Commander of a Fleet
Admiral / Admiral
Vizeadmiral / Vice-Admiral
Konteradmiral / Rear Admiral
Kapitän zur See / Captain
Fregattenkapitän / Commander
Korvettenkapitän / Lieutenant Commander
Kapitänleutnant / Lieutenant
Oberleutnant zur See / Lieutenant (Junior Grade)
Leutnant zur See / Ensign

OFFIZIERSNAHWUCHS / OFFICER CANDIDATES
Oberfahnrich zur See / Senior Midshipman
Fahnrich zur See / Midshipman
Seekadett / Naval Cadet
Matrose (Seeoffiziersanwärter) / Seaman (officer's apprentice)

OFFIZIERE OHNE PATENT / NON-COMMISSIONED OFFICERS
Oberbootsmann / Chief Petty Officer, Chief Boatswain's Mate
Bootsmann / Petty Officer, first class; Boatswain's Mate, first class
Oberbootsmaat / Petty Officer, second class: Boatswain's Mate, second class
Bootsmaat / Petty Officer, third class; Coxswain
Stabobermaschinist / Chief Machinist
Obermaschinist / Warrant Machinist

MANNSCHAFTEN / ENLISTED PERSONNEL
Maschinenmaat / Fireman, first class
Maschinenobergefreiter / Fireman, second class
Maschinengefreiter / Fireman, third class
Oberstabmatrose; Haupgefreiter / Able Seaman, first class
Stabsmatrose, Matrosenobergefreiter, Mechanikerobergefreiter, Funkgefreiter / Seaman, first class
Obermatrose, Matrosengefreiter, Mechaniker-gefreiter, Funkgefreiter / Seaman, second class
Matrose / Seaman, Recruit (apprentice)
Obersteurmann / Navigator
Mechaniker / Artificer's Mate, first class; Torpedoman's Mate, first class
Obermechanikersmaat / Artificer's Mate, second class; Torpedoman's Mate, second class
Mechanikersmaat / Artificer's Mate, third class; Torpedoman's Mate, third class
Oberfunkmaat / Radioman, second class
Funkmaat / Radioman, third class

WOLFPACK
CONCEPT, DEVELOPMENT, PRIMARY RESEARCH, COLOUR PHOTOGRAPHY AND BOOK DESIGN BY PHILIP KAPLAN

TEXT BY JACK CURRIE

PICTURE CREDITS
Photographs by Philip Kaplan are credited: PK. Photos from the author's collections are credited: AC. Jacket front: IWM; jacket back: PK. Jacket back flap, PHILIP KAPLAN: Margaret Kaplan; JACK CURRIE: PK. Title page: Julius Schmitz-Westerholt. FORTY-FOUR SWEATING SEAMEN P6: Charles Eshelman, P7: PK, P8: AC, P9: Bundesarchiv, P10: Bundesarchiv, P11: AC, P12-13, all: Bundesarchiv, P14: PK, P15, top: Bundesarchiv, bottom: AC, P16: Bundesarchiv. THE NARROW DRUM P19: US Army Art Collection, P20: Bundesarchiv, P22, all: AC, P23: IWM, P24: Bundesarchiv, P25: AC, P26: PK, P27: AC. THE LION P28: AC, P30: PK, P31: IWM, P32: AC, P34, left: AC, right: Ryan Cassidy, P35: AC, P36: AC, P38, all: PK, P39, both: AC, P40: Bundesarchiv. EELS, HEDGEHOGS AND SQUIDS P42: IWM, P44: Bundesarchiv, P45: Bundesarchiv, P46, both: PK, P47: IWM, P48: AC, P49: IWM, P50: AC, P51: AC, P53: AC. SUPPLY LINES: P54: AC, P55: US Army Art Collection, P56: US Naval Institute, P58, both: AC, P61: British Film Institute, P62: IWM, P63, both: AC, P64: IWM, P66, top: AC, bottom: IWM, P67, all: AC. TYPE VIIC P68: Bundesarchiv, P69: Bundesarchiv, P70, all: PK, P72: Bernard & Graefe Verlag, P74: Bundesarchiv, P75: PK, P76: Bundesarchiv, P78: PK, P79: US Army Art Collection. HERR KALEU P80: AC, P82, both: PK, P84, left: AC, top: Bundesarchiv, bottom: Ubootarchiv, P85, top left: Ubootarchiv, top right: Bundesarchiv, bottom left: Bundesarchiv, bottom right: AC, P86: US Army Art Collection, P88: Bundesarchiv, P90: AC, P91: PK courtesy Ubootarchiv, P92: Bundesarchiv, P93: Bundesarchiv, P94-95: Malcolm Fisher, P96: AC, P97: Bundesarchiv. THE PENS P98: PK, P100, top: Bundesarchiv, bottom: IWM, P101: AC, P102: US Army Art Collection, P104: Bundesarchiv, P105, both: Bundesarchiv, P106, both: USAF, P107: USAF, P108-109, all: Library of Congress-Frissell Collection-LC-F9-02-4501-039-11, LC-F9-02-4501-010-03, LC-F9-02-4501-060-10, LC-F9-02-4501-057-3, LC-F9-02-4501-054-9, LC-F9-02-4501-013-3, LC-F9-02-4501-073-8, LC-F9-02-4501-059-7, P110, all: PK, P111, all: PK, P112: IWM, P113: IWM. THE HUNT P114: Bundesarchiv, P116: US Naval Institute, P118: Bundesarchiv,

P119: PK, P120: Bundesarchiv, P121, top: Bundesarchiv, bottom: US Coast Guard, P122: IWM, P123: PK, P124: AC, P125: Bundesarchiv, P126: PK. ALARRRM! P128: Bundesarchiv, P130: AC, P131: PK, P132: US Coast Guard, P134: Bundesarchiv, P135: Bundesarchiv. MADDENING ROUTINE P137: Bundesarchiv, P138: PK, P139: AC, P140, left: US Naval Institute, right: Bundesarchiv, P142, top: Bundesarchiv, bottom: British Film Institute-Neue Constantin Film, P143: Bundesarchiv, P144: Bundesarchiv. THE RUSSIAN RUN P147: National Maritime Museum London, P148: IWM, P151: National Maritime Museum London, P152: US Coast Guard, P154: IWM, P156: Bundesarchiv. AT LIBERTY P158: AC, P159: Bundesarchiv, P160: PK, P161: Bundesarchiv, P162: AC, P163, all: PK, P164: Bundesarchiv, P166, top: Ubootarchiv, bottom: Bundesarchiv, P167: Bundesarchiv. MORS AB ALTO P169: US Naval Institute, P170: PK, P171, top: AC, bottom: IWM, P172, top: US Naval Institute, bottom: Michael O'Leary, P174: National Maritime Museum London, P176: US Coast Guard, P177: US Coast Guard, P178: US Coast Guard, P179: AC, P180, left: Bundesarchiv, right: AC, P183: US Coast Guard, P184: US Coast Guard. LOSING IT P187: US Army Art Collection, P189: IWM, P190: US Army Art Collection, P192: AC, P195: USAF, P196: IWM, P198: PK, P201: US Naval Institute, P202, left and bottom: PK, top: Courtesy of Woburn Abbey, P203, top: PK, bottom: Bundesarchiv, P204, both: AC, P205: US Naval Institute, P206: US Navy, P208: Royal Navy Submarine Museum, P210, top: US Naval Institute, bottom: Bundesarchiv, P211: US Naval Institute, P212: AC, P214: US Coast Guard, P215: US Coast Guard, P216: Royal Navy Submarine Museum. U-BOAT P218, both: PK, P219: PK, P220: Bundesarchiv, P222: Bundesarchiv, P223, all: PK, P224: US Naval Institute, P225: PK, P226, top: Bundesarchiv, bottom: PK, P227: PK, P228: US Naval Institute, P230: PK, P231: Shropshire Regimental Museum.

ACKNOWLEDGEMENTS

Special thanks to Margaret Kaplan, Kate Currie and Herta Crull for all the help they gave. We thank the following people whose generous assistance has contributed greatly to the development of this book: Pauline Allwright, Malcolm Bates, Lance Bauserman, Beverley Brannan, Horst Bredow, Geoffrey Brooks, R.M. Browning, Jr., Piers Burnett, Brian Burns, Ryan Cassidy, Harry Cooper, Debby Corner, Jane Costantini, The Dark Room, Captain A.C.Douglas, Lee Edwards, Charles Eshelman, Gary Fisher/Butec, Ella Freire, Oz Freire, Betty Hamilton, Ed Holm, Franc Isla, John James, Claire Kaplan, Joseph Kaplan, Neal Kaplan, Paul Kemp, Judy McCutcheon, Richard McCutcheon, James McMaster, Tilly McMaster, Hans Milkert, Michael O'Leary, Prom, Susan Roth, Vern Schwartz, Lloyd Stovall, Mary Beth Straight, John Zinner.

Thanks too, to Robin Watson, ex-Royal Navy submariner, and Fiona Andrews, for their help, respectively, regarding submarines and the German language, and to Malcolm Fisher for permitting the showing of the Günther Prien awards (pages 94–95). The Prien items are available for sale by Mr Fisher who may be contacted at 70 Essex Road, Islington, London N1 8LT, England.

BIBLIOGRAPHY

Beaver, Paul, *U-Boats in the Atlantic*, Patrick Stephens Ltd, 1979.
Bekker, Cajus, *The German Navy 1939–1945*, Dial Press, 1974.
Botting, Douglas, *The U-Boats*, Time-Life Books–The Seafarers, 1979.
Broome, Jack, *Convoy Is To Scatter*, William Kimber, 1972.
Buchheim, Lothar-Günther, *The Boat*, William Collins, 1976.
Cantwell, John C., *Images of War–British Posters 1939–45*, HMSO.
Clancy, Tom, *Submarine*, Berkley Books, 1993.
Cremer, Peter, *U-Boat Commander*, Naval Institute Press, 1985.
Crowther, J.G. & Whiddington, R., *Science At War*, HMSO, 1947.
Dönitz, Karl, *Memoirs*, Greenill Books, 1990.
Enever, Ted, *Britain's Best Kept Secret–Ultra's Base At Bletchley Park*, Alan Sutton, 1994.
Farrago, Ladislas, *The Tenth Fleet*, Drum Books, 1962.
Gallery, Daniel V., *Twenty Million Tons Under The Sea*, Regnery, 1956.
Gannon, Michael, *Operation Drumbeat*, Harper Perennial, 1990.
Giese, Otto, *Shooting The War*, Naval Institute Press, 1994.
Gray, Edwin, *The Killing Time*, Scribners, 1972.
Guske, Heinz F.K., *The War Diaries of U-764*, Thomas Publications, 1992.
Hadley, Michael L., *Count Not The Dead*, Naval Institute Press, 1995.
Hampshire, A. Cecil, *The Blockaders*, William Kimber, 1980.
Harris, M.R.A.F. Sir Arthur, *Bomber Offensive*, Collins, 1937.
Harris, M.R.A.F. Sir Arthur, *Bomber Offensive*, Collins, 1947.
Hickam, Homer H., *Torpedo Junction*, Naval Institute Press, 1989.
HMSO, *The Battle of the Atlantic*, 1946.
HMSO, *Coastal Command*, 1942.
HMSO, *We Speak From The Air*, 1942.
Hough, Richard, *The Longest Battle*, Weidenfeld & Nicolson, 1986.
Horton, Edward, *The Illustrated History of the Submarine*, Sidgewick and Jackson, 1974.
Hoyt, Edwin P., *The U-Boat Wars*, Robert Hale Ltd, 1984.
Humble, R. & Bergin, M., *A WWII Submarine*,

The impulse to mar and to destroy is as ancient and almost as nearly universal as the impulse to create. The one is an easier way than the other of demonstrating power.
—from *The Best of Two Worlds*
by Joseph Wood Krutch

The last pleasure in life is the sense of discharging our duty.
—from *Characteristics* by William Hazlitt

below: A Dom-bunker at the Lorient base.

Naval Institute Press, 1991.
Jackson, G. Gibbard, *The Romance of a Submarine*, J.B. Lippincott.
John Jahr Verlag, *Waffen im Einsatz*, 1976.
Jones, Geoffrey, *Defeat of the Wolf Packs*, William Kimber, 1986.
Jones, Geoffrey, *Submarines Versus U-Boats*, William Kimber, 1986.
Kemp, Paul, *Convoy Protection*, Arms & Armour, 1993.
Kemp, P.K., *H.M.Submarines*, Herbert Jenkins, 1952.
Lamb, Charles, *To War in a Stringbag*, Nelson Doubleday, 1977.
Lewin, Ronald, *Ultra Goes To War*, McGraw-Hill, 1978.
Lund, Paul & Ludham, Harry, *Night of the U-Boats*, NEL, 1974.
Macintyre, Donald, *The Battle of the Atlantic*, Pan Books, 1961.
Margolin, V., *Propaganda: Persuasion in WWII Art*, Chelsea House, 1976.
Miller, David & Jordan, John, *Modern Submarine Warfare*, Salamander Books, 1987.
Mason, David, *U-Boat: The Secret Menace*, Ballantine Books, 1968.
Messenger, Charles, *World War II in the Atlantic*, Warfare Books and Toys Ltd., 1990.
Middlebrook, Martin, and Everitt, Chris, *The Bomber Command War Diaries,* Penguin, 1990.
Middlebrook, Martin, *Convoy*, Penguin Books, 1978.
MoD, *The U-Boat War in the Atlantic*, HMSO, 1989.
Morison, Samuel Eliot, *The Battle of the Atlantic, Volume One*, Little Brown, 1947.
Mulligan, Thomas P., *Lone Wolf-Werner Henke*, Praeger, 1993.
Murrow, Edward R., *This Is London*, Shocken Books, 1941.
Neitzel, Sonke, *Die Deutschen Ubootbunker und Bunkerwerften*, Bernard & Graefe Verlag, 1991.
Pitt, Barrie, *The Battle of the Atlantic*, Time-Life Books, 1977.
Robertson, Terence, *The Golden Horseshoe*, Evans Brothers, 1955.
Rossler, Eberhard, *The U-Boat*, Naval Institute Press, 1989.
Runyan, Timothy & Copes, Jan M., *To Die Gallantly*, Westview Press, 1994.
Showell, Jak P. Mallmann, *The German Navy in WWII*, Naval Institute Press, 1991.
Showell, Jak P. Mallmann, *U-Boats Under the Swastika*, Naval Institute Press, 1989.
Syrett, David, *The Defeat of the German U-Boats*, U. of S. Carolina, 1994.
Tarrant, V.E., *The U-Boat Offensive 1914–1945*, Naval Institute Press, 1989.

The U-Boat Commander's Handbook, Thomas Publications, 1989.
Vause, Jordan, *U-Boat Ace: Wolfgang Lüth*, Naval Institute Press, 1976.
Warlimont, Walter, *Inside Hitler's Headquarters 1939–45*, Presidio Press, 1993.
Waters, John M., *Bloody Winter,* Naval Institute Press, 1967.
Werner, Herbert, *Iron Coffins*, Holt, Rinehart & Winston, 1969.
Westwood, David, *The Type VII U-Boat*, Naval Institute Press, 1984.
Winton, John, *Ultra At Sea*, Leo Cooper, 1988.

INDEX